CW01162974

The
MOCKTAIL HOUR

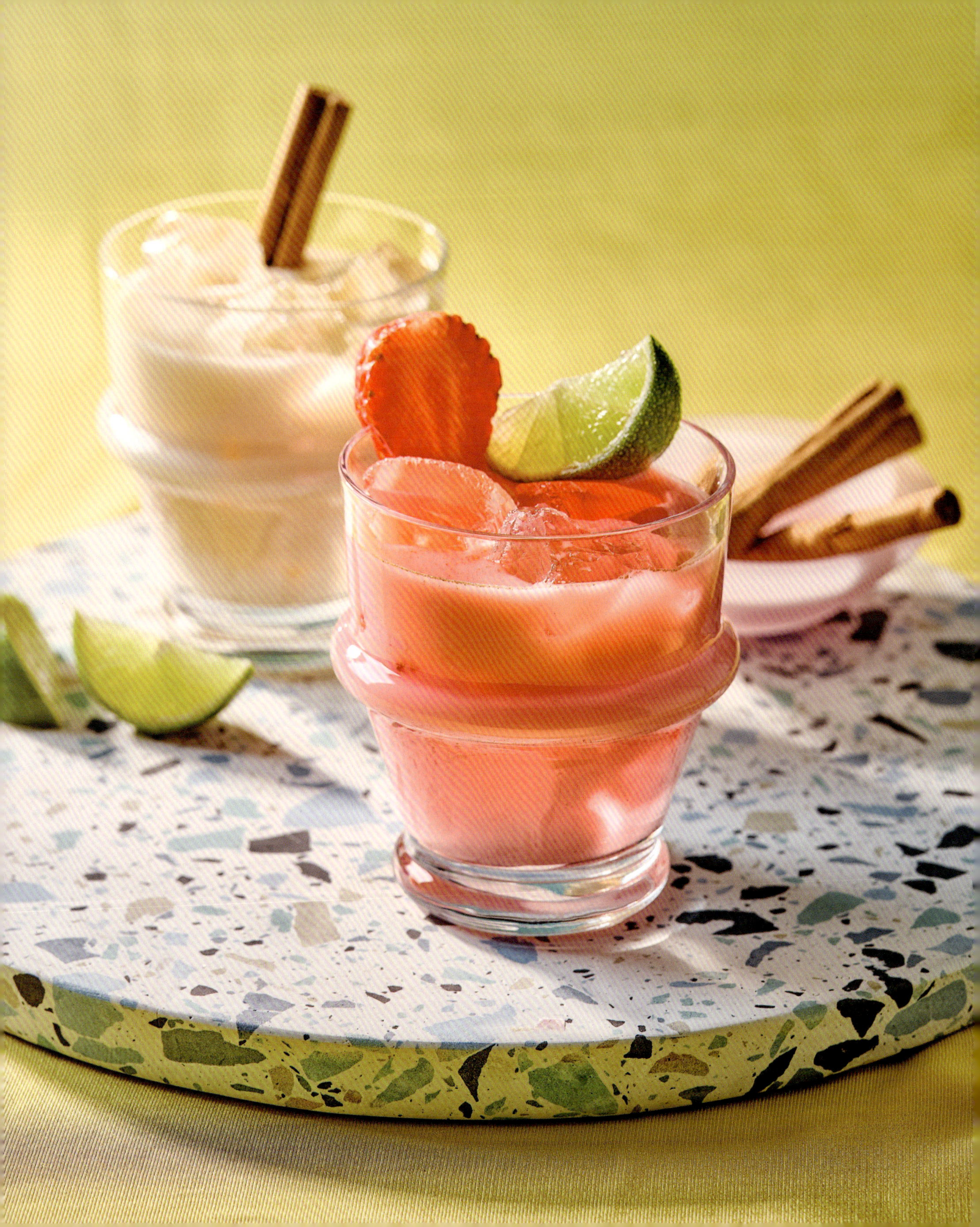

The
MOCKTAIL HOUR

*Deliciously different zero-proof
drinks for the sober curious*

DAVID T. SMITH & KELI RIVERS

with photography by Tim Atkins

RYLAND PETERS & SMALL

DEDICATION

To The Bear and whomever mixed me my first mocktail as child (in a Beefeater pub).

'If you want a thing done well, get a couple of old broads to do it.' What do you say Ms. Nance, fancy a go?

Senior Designer Toni Kay
Copy Editor Kate Reeves-Brown
Production Manager Gordana Simakovic
Editorial Director Julia Charles
Creative Director Leslie Harrington

Prop Stylist Luis Peral
Drinks Stylist Katherine Lunt
Indexer Vanessa Bird

First published in 2025 by
Ryland Peters & Small
20–21 Jockey's Fields, London
WC1R 4BW
and
1452 Davis Bugg Road
Warrenton, NC 27589

www.rylandpeters.com
email: euregulations@rylandpeters.com

10 9 8 7 6 5 4 3 2 1

Text © David T. Smith & Keli Rivers 2025
Design and commissioned photography © Ryland Peters & Small 2025, see page 128 for full image credits.

Printed and bound in China.

The authors' moral rights have been asserted. All rights reserved. No part of this publication may be reproduced, stored in a retrieval system or transmitted in any form or by any means, electronic, mechanical, photocopying or otherwise, without the prior permission of the publisher.

ISBN: 978-1-78879-726-9

A CIP record for this book is available from the British Library. US Library of Congress cataloging-in-Publication Data has been applied for.

The authorised representative in the EEA is Authorised Rep Compliance Ltd., Ground Floor, 71 Lower Baggot Street, Dublin, D02 P593, Ireland www.arccompliance.com

NOTES

• All spoon measurements are level unless otherwise specified. A teaspoon is 5 ml and a tablespoon is 15 ml.
• When a recipe calls for the peel or grated zest of citrus fruit, buy unwaxed fruit and wash well before using.
• Uncooked or partially cooked eggs should not be served to the very old, frail, young children, pregnant women or those with compromised immune systems.

CONTENTS

Introduction	6
HAPPY HOUR HEROES	10
TROPICAL TREATS	36
PORCH DRINKS	50
THE SODA FOUNTAIN	74
PICK-ME-UPS	88
SEASONAL SPECIALS	108
Basic Recipes	122
Index	126
Acknowledgements & credits	128

INTRODUCTION

Mocktails, non-alcoholic, no & low, soft drinks, dry drinks, zero-proof, 0.0% and temperance are all terms for a category of drink that is becoming increasingly popular: alcohol-free drinks.

Some of these terms feel a tad too sterile and lifeless, so for this book we use the term 'mocktails', as it's more fun, and drinks – whatever their ABV – should at least be that.

Let's picture the scene that's all too familiar: a bar, a pub or a restaurant where great care and attention is given to the alcoholic drinks, but the non-alcoholic ones are just sploshed into a glass without a second thought. The most basic of glassware, no garnish, barely any ice. If the drink is bottled, it might not have even been kept in the fridge! If you are on the receiving end of such a mediocre libation, you can't help feeling that you've drawn the short straw.

There is one, simple rule for a successful mocktail: spend as much time and effort on a non-alcoholic drink as you would on an alcoholic one.

COOL BUBBLES: CHILL & CARBONATION

Many of the recipes in this book call for the use of carbonated ingredients, either from a bottle or a can. Here some considerations:

1. *It's important to keep the drinks cold before use. This boosts effervescence, ensuring that they are fizzier when poured, and also accentuates the drier flavours, which can stop a drink from becoming too sweet. Even if you add a glacier of ice to a drink, it can't fully compensate for chilling the ingredients first.*

2. *Once open, carbonated products can quickly lose their fizz, so, unless you are planning on making lots of drinks in quick succession, the use of individual servings (for example miniature cans) of fizzy drinks are best. That way, it can be fresh for every drink.*

THE TALE OF NO & LOW

Non-alcoholic drinks (even outside of tea and coffee) have existed for centuries. In places where running water was not readily available, fresh, clean water could require considerable effort to acquire, and therefore it makes sense that this precious resource would often be enhanced with other flavours such as fruit, fruit juice, flowers and herbs.

Examples include: agua fresca and horchata from Mexico, limonana from the Levant, lassi from India, and iced tea in the USA.

It can also be seen in the nostalgic lemonade stands of yesteryear, where children started with some basic, raw ingredients and were taught how to combine them to add value and (hopefully) make a profit.

The early 20th century saw a growing temperance movement in the US (and elsewhere), which saw in the rise of temperance bars and temperance drinks (essentially non-alcoholic drinks). There was an accompanying rise in 'soda fountains' or 'soda shops', which were found in US drug stores or pharmacies, and operated by soda 'jerks'.

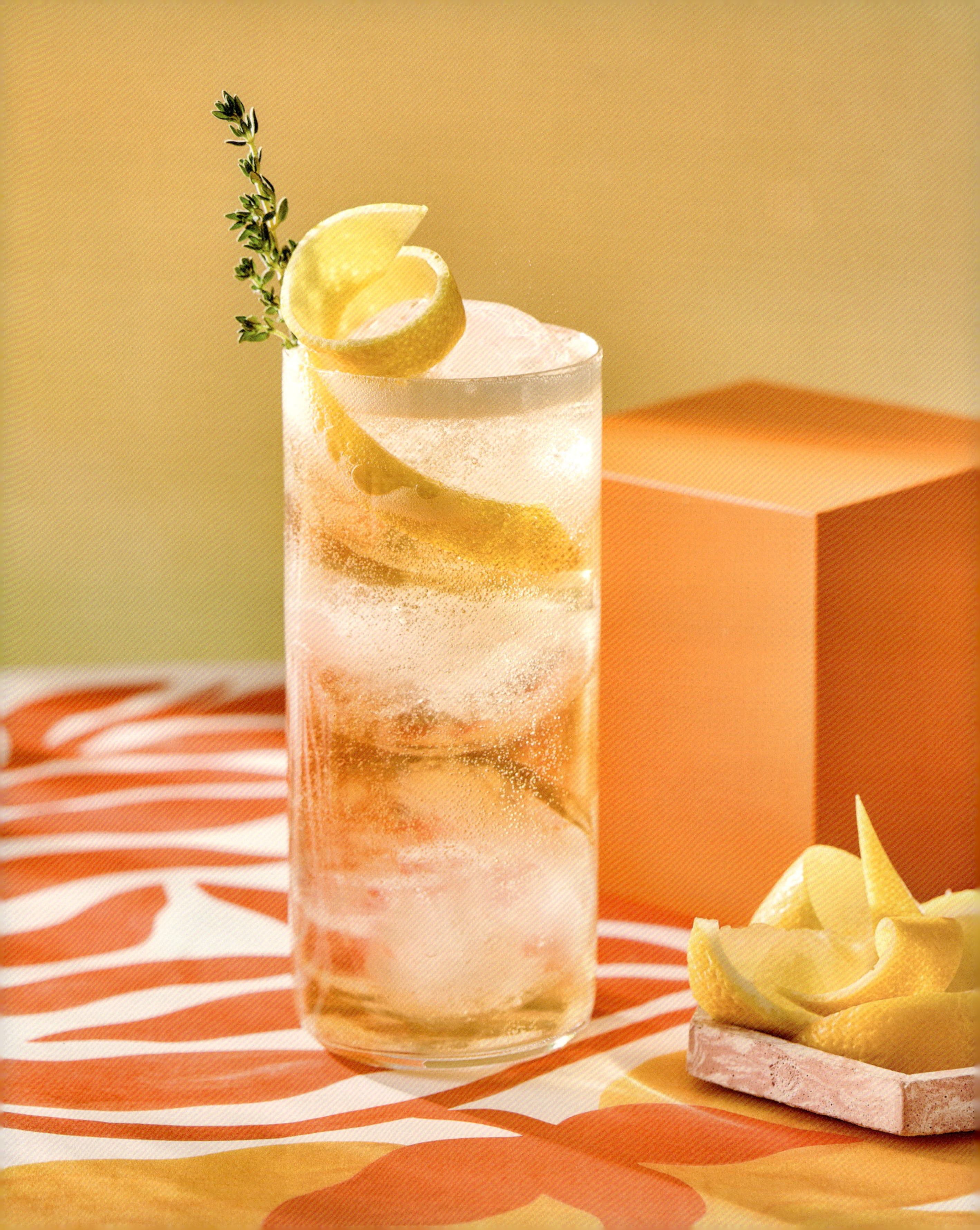

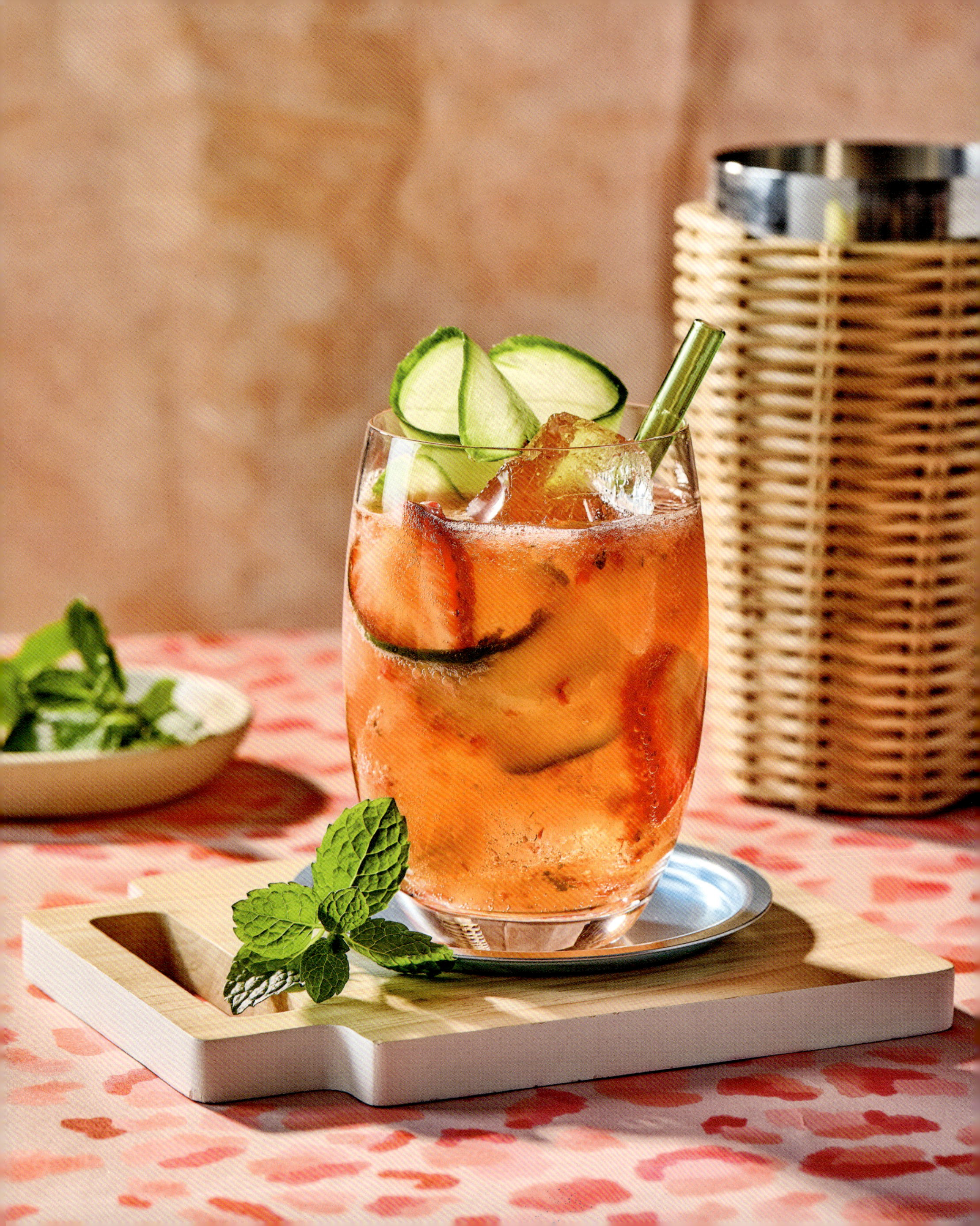

At the same time, more and more brands of fizzy or carbonated drinks (sodas) were achieving national and international distribution. For Coca-Cola, the temperance bar was actually instrumental in cementing their place in the modern psyche (which is somewhat ironic, as, today, Coca-Cola is one of the most popular mixers for alcoholic drinks).

In 1920, the 18th Amendment to the United States Constitution was passed and the legal manufacture, sale and transportation of alcoholic beverages was banned. This led to the soda shop replacing many bars as legitimate social meeting spots. However, drug stores were also one of the few places that could legally sell alcohol (for medicinal reasons) and so the concoctions at the soda bar could be a convenient way to disguise the serving of alcohol.

Around this time, illicit 'speakeasies' started to open, serving alcoholic drinks to a sympathetic clientele. With supply lines often disrupted, drinkers had to take what they could get and the quality of the alcohol sometimes suffered. This led to a fresh boom in new cocktails that both helped to disguise what was being drunk and made any inferior spirits more palatable.

Also responding to the times, a number of American brewers embarked on a quest to create 'near beer': a brewed malt-based beverage with a final alcoholic strength of less than 0.5% ABV. Importantly, such a product could still be legally sold during Prohibition. This laid the foundation for many of the 'no & low' beers that are available today.

THE MODERN PHASE

Things trundled along for a bit – a non-alcoholic beer here, a de-alcoholised wine there – but little else impacted the world of the mocktail beyond the invention of diet sodas and the proliferation of artificial sweeteners.

In 2014, this changed with the launch of Seedlip, a botanically distilled product that contains no alcohol. Despite its use of botanicals, it was not designed to be a direct replacement for gin, but it could be used to mix non-alcoholic cocktails and could be found in the alcohol section of shops. In the decade that followed, there was a huge increase in the variety and quality of non-alcoholic 'spirits'. Alternatives for gin, rum, whisky, tequila, vermouth and bitters are all now more readily available and, without them, a book of this nature couldn't exist.

THE MOCKTAIL HOUR is divided into chapters, with each one focusing on drinks for different occasions or with different flavour profiles:

Happy Hour Heroes focuses on direct non-alcoholic counterparts for some of the world's most popular cocktails.

Tropical Treats features sun-kissed, exotic flavours and long, chilled coolers.

Porch Drinks has a host of easy-going recipes designed for relaxed socializing and sippin'.

The Soda Fountain contains old-school treats and ice-cream floats with a modern twist.

Pick-Me-Ups presents an array of coffee and cola focused drinks for that little caffeine buzz.

Seasonal Specials features mocktails for all kinds of special occasions.

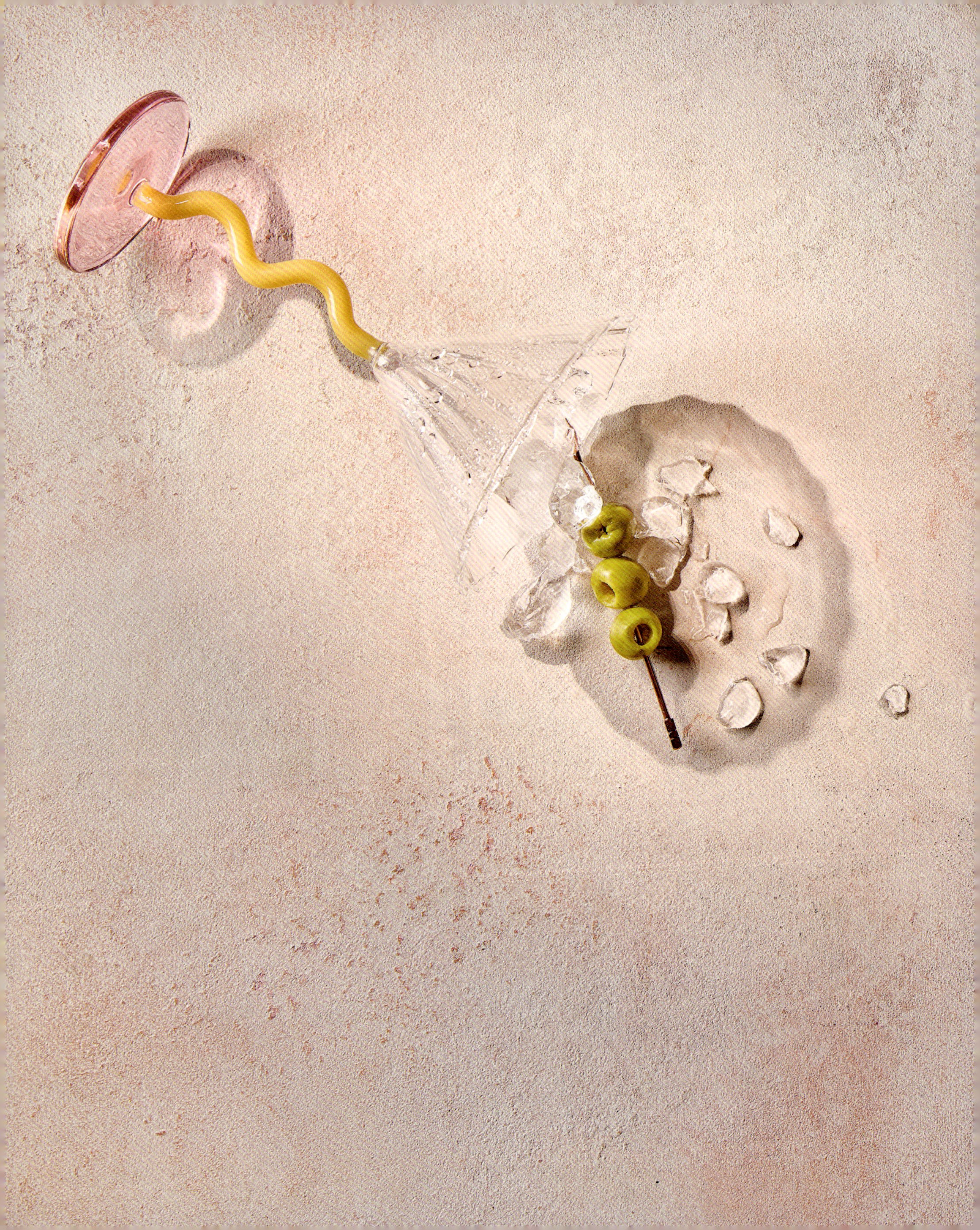

HAPPY HOUR HEROES

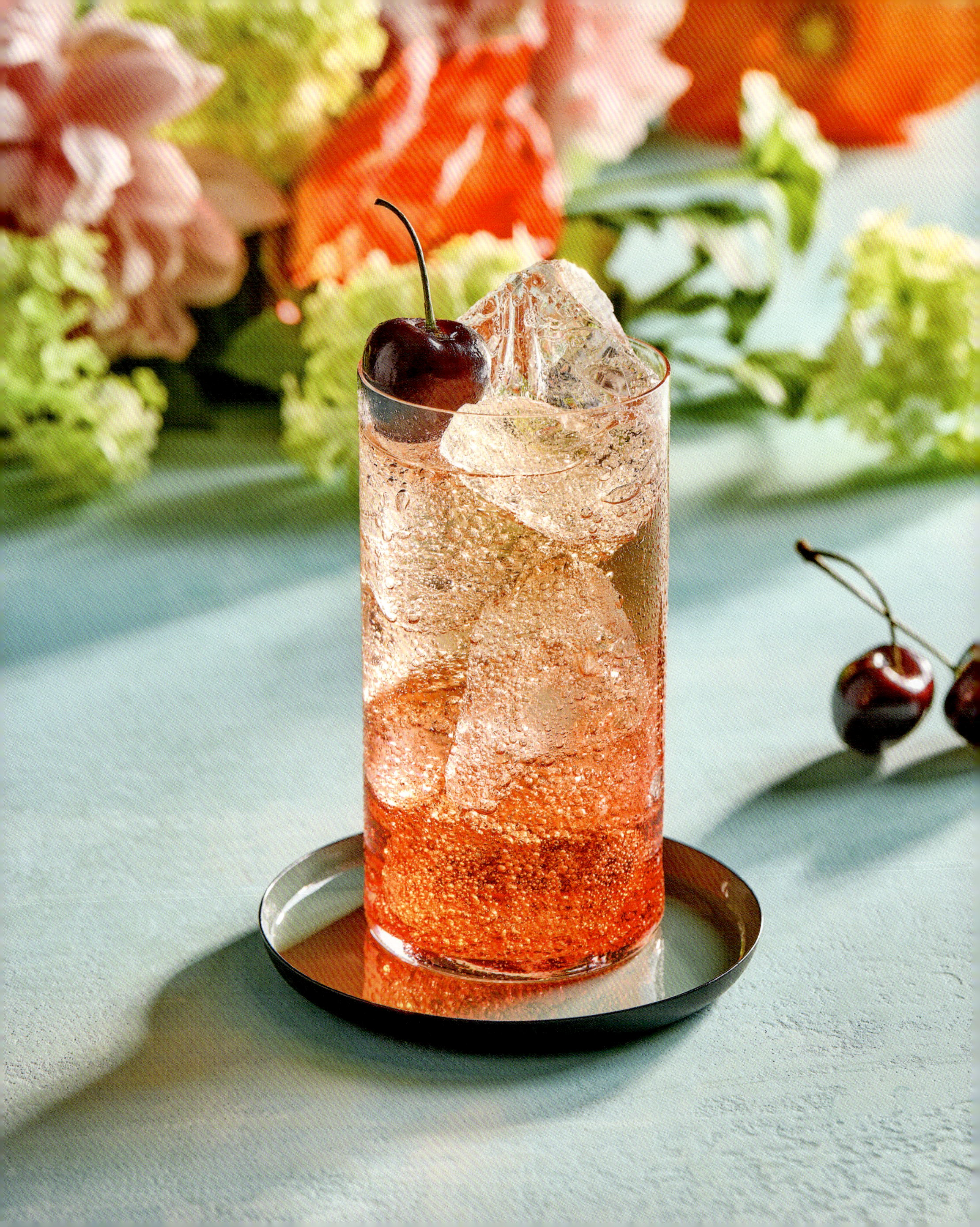

SHIRLEY TEMPLE

This drink was created in the 1930s for the child star after she lamented that she couldn't have her parents' Old Fashioneds, which were still being made with neon red maraschino cherries. Bartenders from a range of venues have all laid claim to its creation, including Hollywood's Chasen's restaurant, the Brown Derby restaurant and even Honolulu's Royal Hawaiian Hotel. Despite the conflicting stories, one thing remains clear: Shirley Temple was served this drink frequently, regardless of her personal dislike for it.

200 ml/7 oz. soda (ginger ale, lemon-lime soda or a 50:50 mix)
25 ml/¾ oz. grenadine
50 ml/1¾ oz. fresh orange juice (optional)
maraschino cherry, to garnish

SERVES 1

Fill a highball glass with ice. Add the soda, and drizzle the grenadine over the top, followed by the orange juice, if using. Garnish with a maraschino cherry.

ROY ROGERS

Known as the King of Cowboys, Roy Rogers got his start as part of the singing group Sons of the Pioneers in 1935, before making his way to the silver screen in the 1940s, where he ended up starring in almost 100 films. This drink originated in the 1940s and was named after this well-known teetotaller, who even has his own chain of restaurants!

180 ml/6 oz. cola, chilled
10–15 ml/⅓–½ oz. grenadine
cocktail cherry, to garnish

SERVES 1

Pour the cola into an ice-filled highball glass and drizzle over the grenadine. Garnish with a cocktail cherry and add a straw.

VARIATION:
For a **Trigger** (the name of Roy Rogers' horse) follow the recipe as above, but add the juice from a wedge of lime to the drink for extra zing and add another lime wedge to garnish.

VIRGIN MARY

The secret to an impressive cocktail is to spend time on presentation and garnish. With the Virgin Mary, this is easy to do, as most of the flavour of its boozy cousin the Bloody Mary comes from the mixer and garnishes.

A rookie error is to put the whole kitchen sink of seasonings into the drink, especially when you first try one. It's better to start with plain tomato juice and then gradually build up the use of seasonings and garnishes. You can serve it how you like, however, this is a go-to recipe that just about strikes the right balance.

500 ml/17 oz. good-quality tomato juice (ideally pressed and not from concentrate)
2 tablespoons Worcestershire sauce
1 tablespoon Sriracha or other hot sauce (optional)
3-cm/1¼-inch piece of fresh horseradish, peeled and finely grated, or 2 teaspoons from a jar
60 ml/2 oz. freshly squeezed lime juice
sea salt and freshly ground black pepper

TO GARNISH
4 celery sticks/ribs
4 lemon wedges
4 cherry tomatoes, halved
4 cocktail sticks/toothpicks

SERVES 4

Combine all of the ingredients in a jug/pitcher and stir gently to combine. Season to taste with salt and pepper and chill until ready to serve. Fill four highball glasses with ice and slowly fill each one with the mix. Garnish each serving with a celery stick (to act as a stirrer), a lemon wedge and a cocktail stick threaded with two cherry tomato halves. Serve at once.

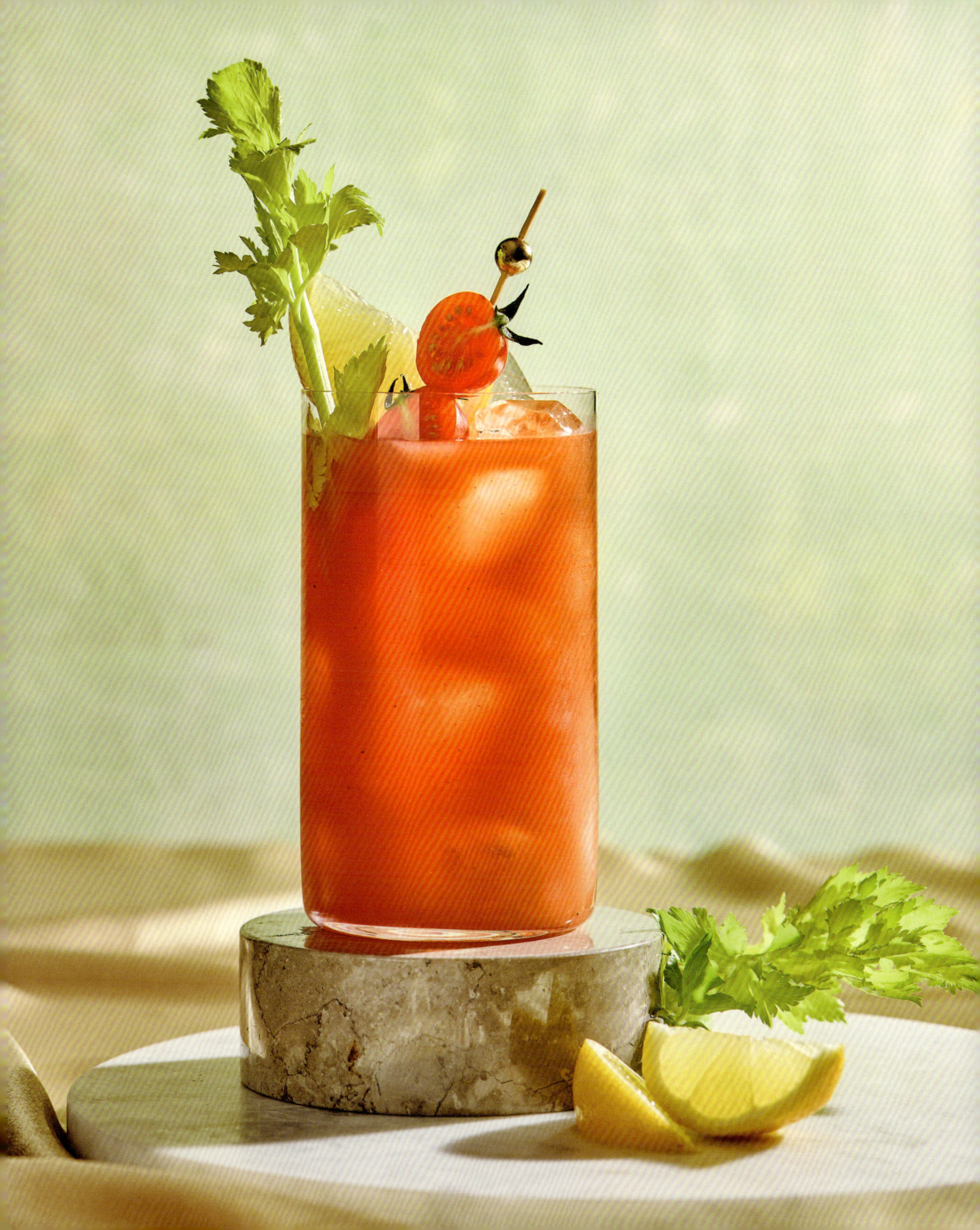

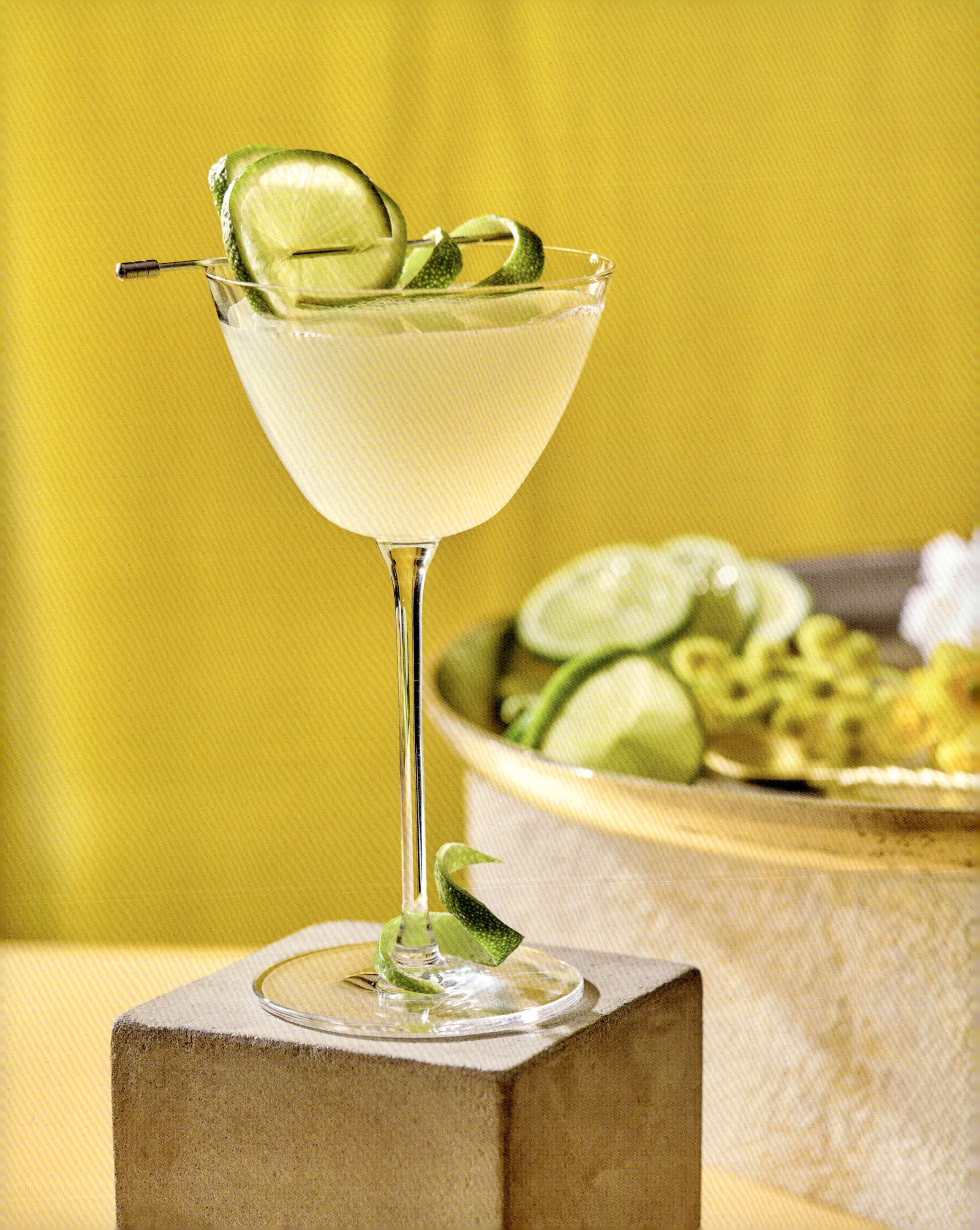

THE DRIVER'S DAIQUIRI

Some mocktails use facsimiles or imitations of spirits such as gin or rum. These are particularly useful for relatively simple drinks such as the Daiquiri. This version uses the Australian Lyre's White Cane Spirit, but other alternatives are available.

The Daiquiri is a combination of 'spirit', sugar and citrus juice. As it belongs to the sours family of drinks, freshly squeezed lime juice (even if it is squeezed in advance) is an essential ingredient.

50 ml/1¾ oz. Lyre's White Cane Spirit
25 ml/¾ oz. freshly squeezed lime juice
20 ml/⅔ oz. Simple Sugar Syrup (see page 123)
lime wheel, to garnish

SERVES 1

Shake the ingredients vigorously in a shaker with ice, and strain into a chilled cocktail glass. Garnish with a wheel of lime.

VARIATIONS:
If you're looking for a little more adventure, try substituting half of the Simple Sugar Syrup with a flavoured one such as Ginger (see page 124) for a **High Tide Daiquiri**, Vanilla (see page 124) for a **Velvet Daiquiri**, or Cherry (see page 78) for a **Ruby Rush**.

MOCKTAIL MOJITO

Another cooling rum-inspired classic. The lime and the mint add a bright zing and cooling freshness, while the soda water brings length and a touch of sparkle. The use of golden or even brown sugar (rather than white) helps to give the drink a richer more rum-like flavour.

1 tablespoon golden caster/superfine sugar
small bunch of mint
freshly squeezed juice of 3 limes
soda water, to top up

SERVES 2

Gently muddle the sugar and mint using a pestle and mortar (or use a small bowl and the end of a rolling pin). Put a handful of crushed ice into 2 tall glasses. Divide the lime juice between the glasses, along with the mint mixture. Add a straw to each glass and top up with soda water.

HAPPY HOUR HEROES

GREY 'N' WINDY

A Dark 'N' Stormy is a classic and refreshing rum drink typically associated with Goslings Rum. This non-alcoholic variation uses tea and cinnamon to evoke some of the woody, spiced complexity of that spirit. The drink does include a few dashes of alcoholic cocktail bitters, but the amount is so small that the relative % ABV of the drink is negligible.

30 ml/1 oz. freshly squeezed lime juice
15 ml/½ oz. Cinnamon Syrup (see page 124)
90 ml/3 oz. cold brew black tea
pinch of sea salt (kosher salt)
ginger beer, as needed
2–4 dashes angostura bitters, to taste
lime wedge, to garnish

SERVES 1

Add all of the ingredients, except the ginger beer and angostura bitters, to a shaker and shake vigorously with ice. Pour the mixture into a tall, ice-filled glass and top-up with the ginger beer. Add the angostura bitters and garnish with a lime wedge.

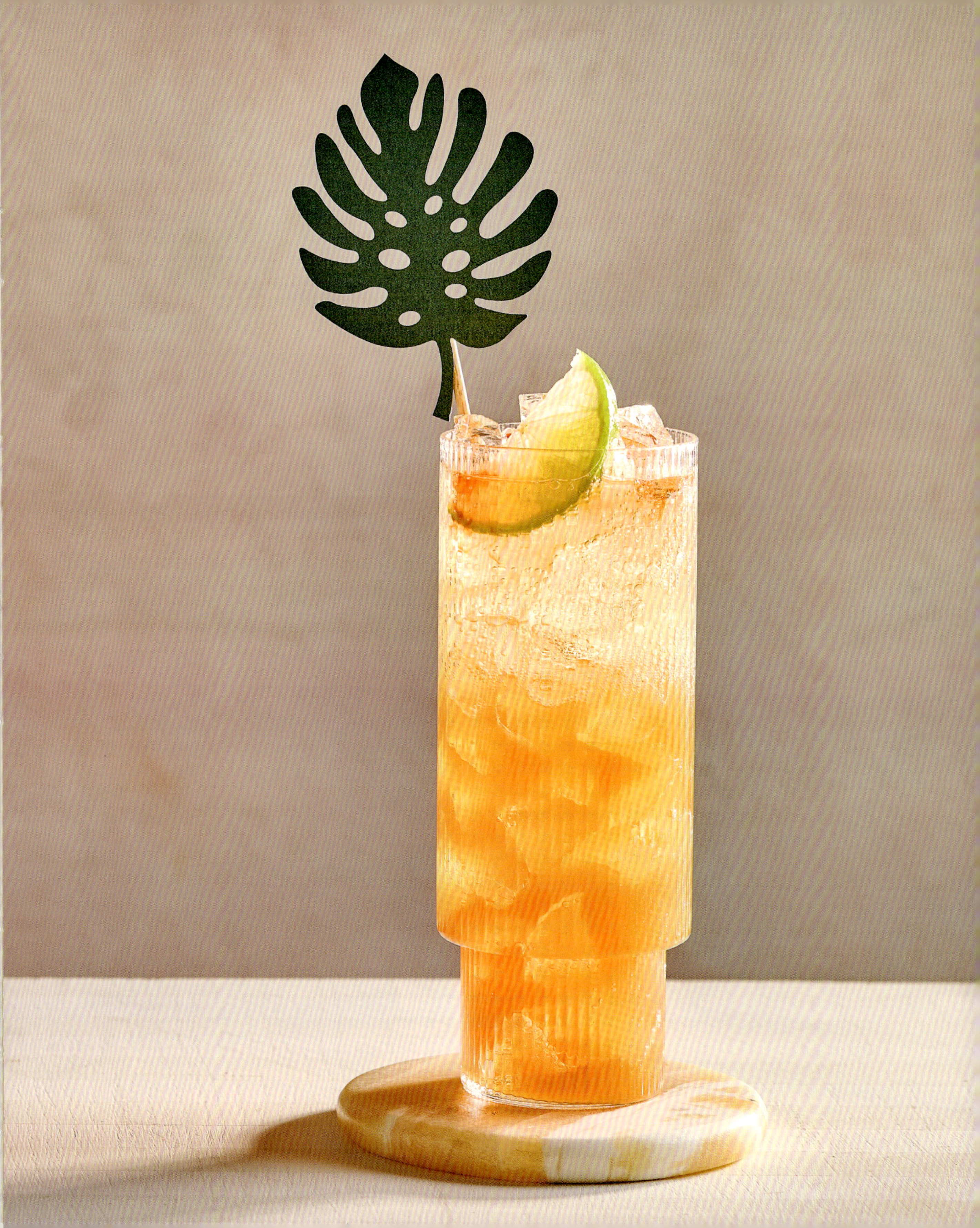

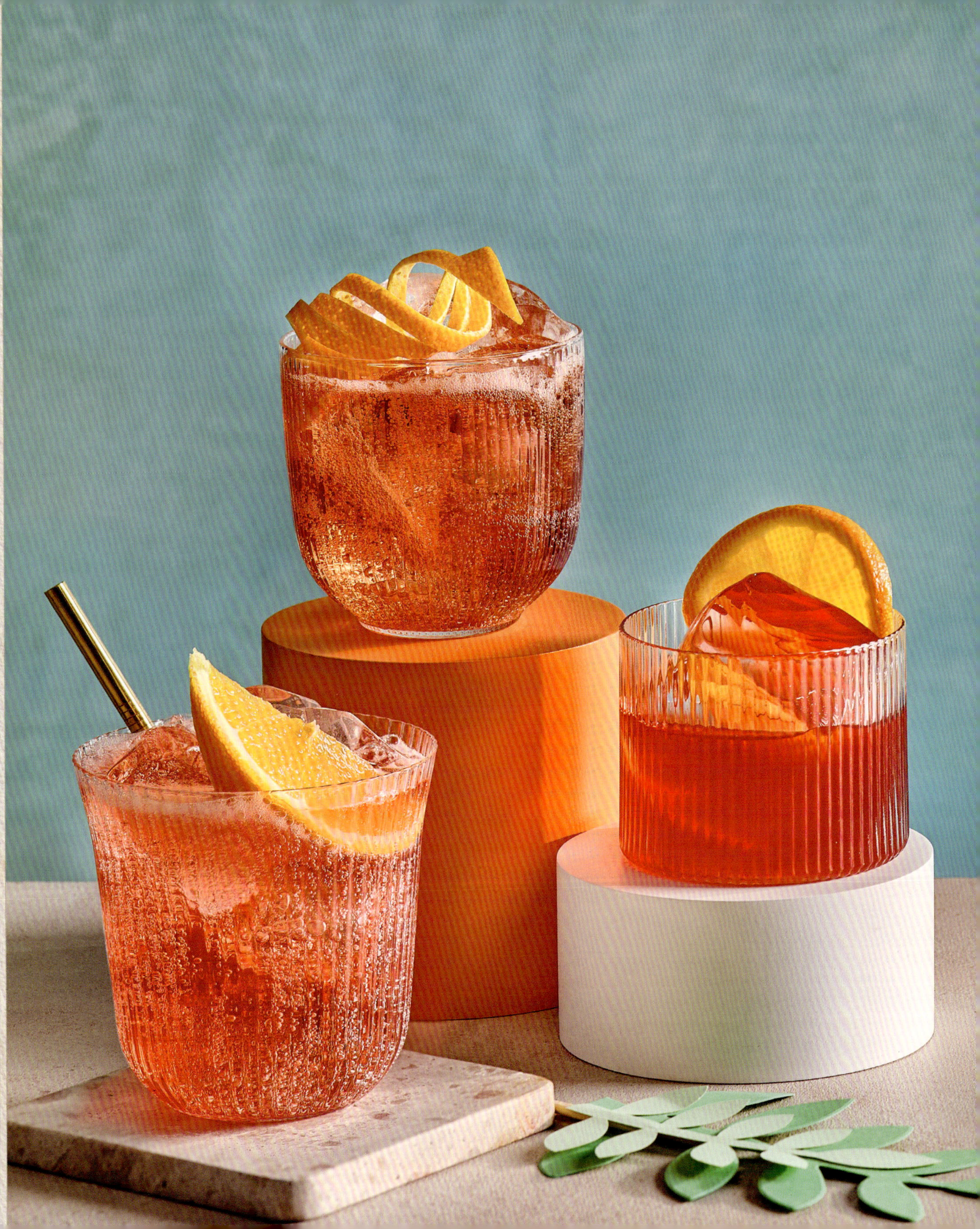

NO-GRONI

No cocktail has risen in popularity in recent years like the Negroni: from near obscurity to a firm favourite, spawning an exciting array of variations. This non-alcoholic version simply uses non-alcoholic substitutes for gin, Campari and vermouth in equal parts.

30 ml/1 oz. Lyre's Italian Orange or other Campari substitute
30 ml/1 oz. gin substitute, such as Tanqueray 0.0%
30 ml/1 oz. vermouth substitute, such as Versin Aperitivo or Martini Aperitivo
lemon or orange wheel, to garnish

SERVES 1

Combine the ingredients in an ice-filled tumbler and stir. Garnish with a lemon or orange wheel.

SBAGLIATO

A booze-free version of the latest Negroni variation to be in vogue; here, the gin is replaced by non-alcoholic sparkling wine.

25 ml/¾ oz. Lyre's Italian Orange or other Campari substitute
25 ml/¾ oz. Versin Aperitivo
25 ml/¾ oz. non-alcoholic sparkling wine, or more as needed
orange peel, to garnish

SERVES 1

Build in an ice-filled tumbler, stir briefly and garnish with orange peel.

AMERICA-NO

The quintessential café cocktail – long, refreshing and ideal for a sunny afternoon. It is also the first drink that James Bond ever orders; so much for the Martini!

25 ml/¾ oz. Lyres Aperitivo
25 ml/¾ oz. Martini Vibrante
100 ml/3¾ oz. sparkling water
orange wedge, to garnish

SERVES 1

Add the ingredients to a tall ice-filled glass. Top up with sparkling water and garnish with an orange wedge. Serve with a swivel stick.

POPSTAR MARTINI

A retro cocktail that first appeared around the turn of the new millennium and has had a recent revival. The original was invented by Douglas Ankrah in 2002. This is a fun and fruity drink that lends itself well to a virgin version.

60 ml/2 oz. passion fruit juice
15 ml/½ oz. freshly squeezed lemon juice
30 ml/1 oz. pineapple Juice
15 ml/½ oz. Vanilla Syrup (see page 124)
30 ml/1 oz. gin substitute, such as Tanqueray 0.0%, Gordon's 0.0% or Sipsmith FreeGlider
30 ml/1 oz. non-alcoholic sparkling wine, chilled, to serve

SERVES 1

Shake the ingredients vigorously with ice and strain into a large V-shaped cocktail glass. Serve with a shot glass of chilled non-alcoholic sparkling wine on the side.

VARIATION:
For a **Popstar Pop**, follow the recipe as above, but pour the shaken mix into a tall, ice-filled glass and top-up with cream soda.

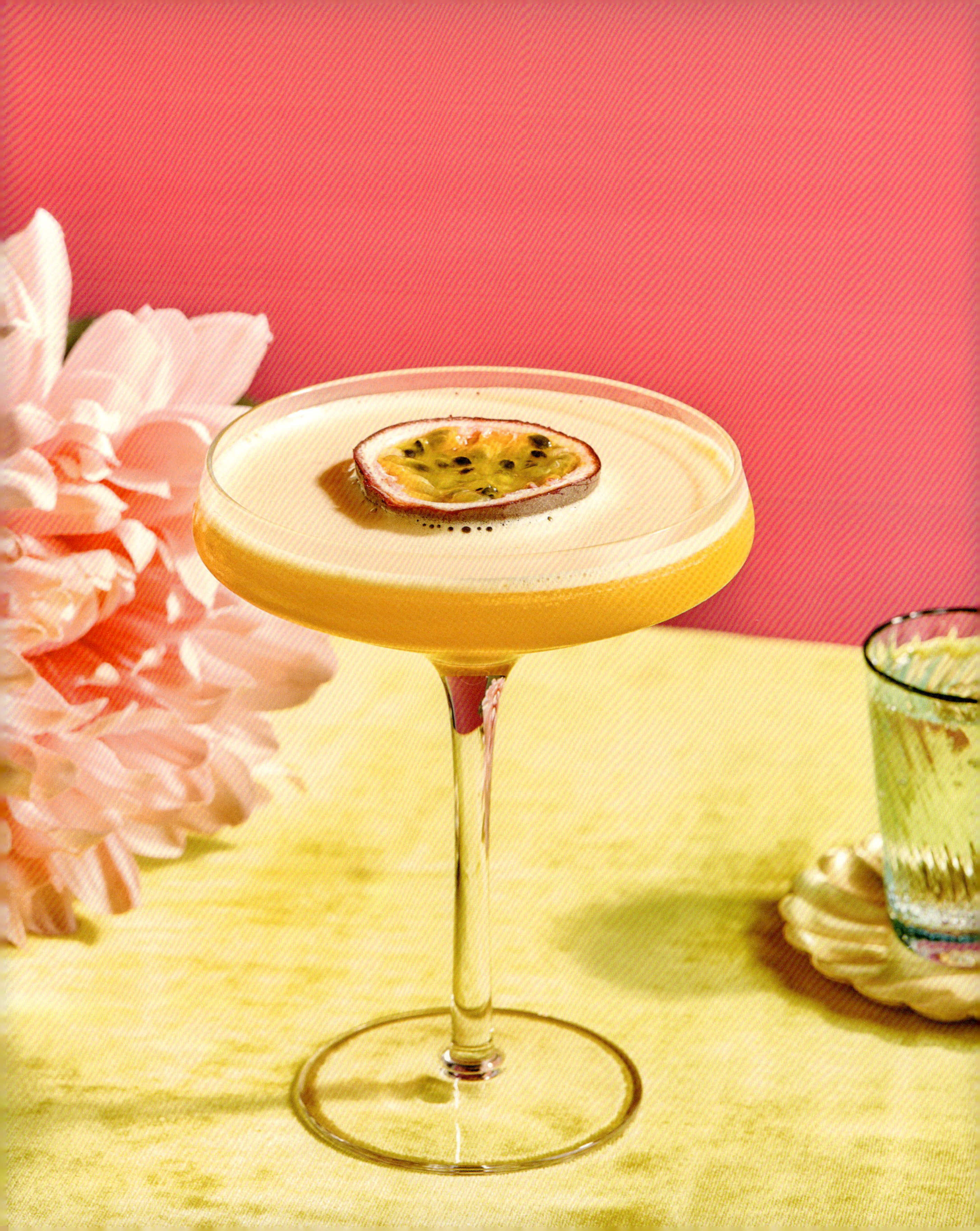

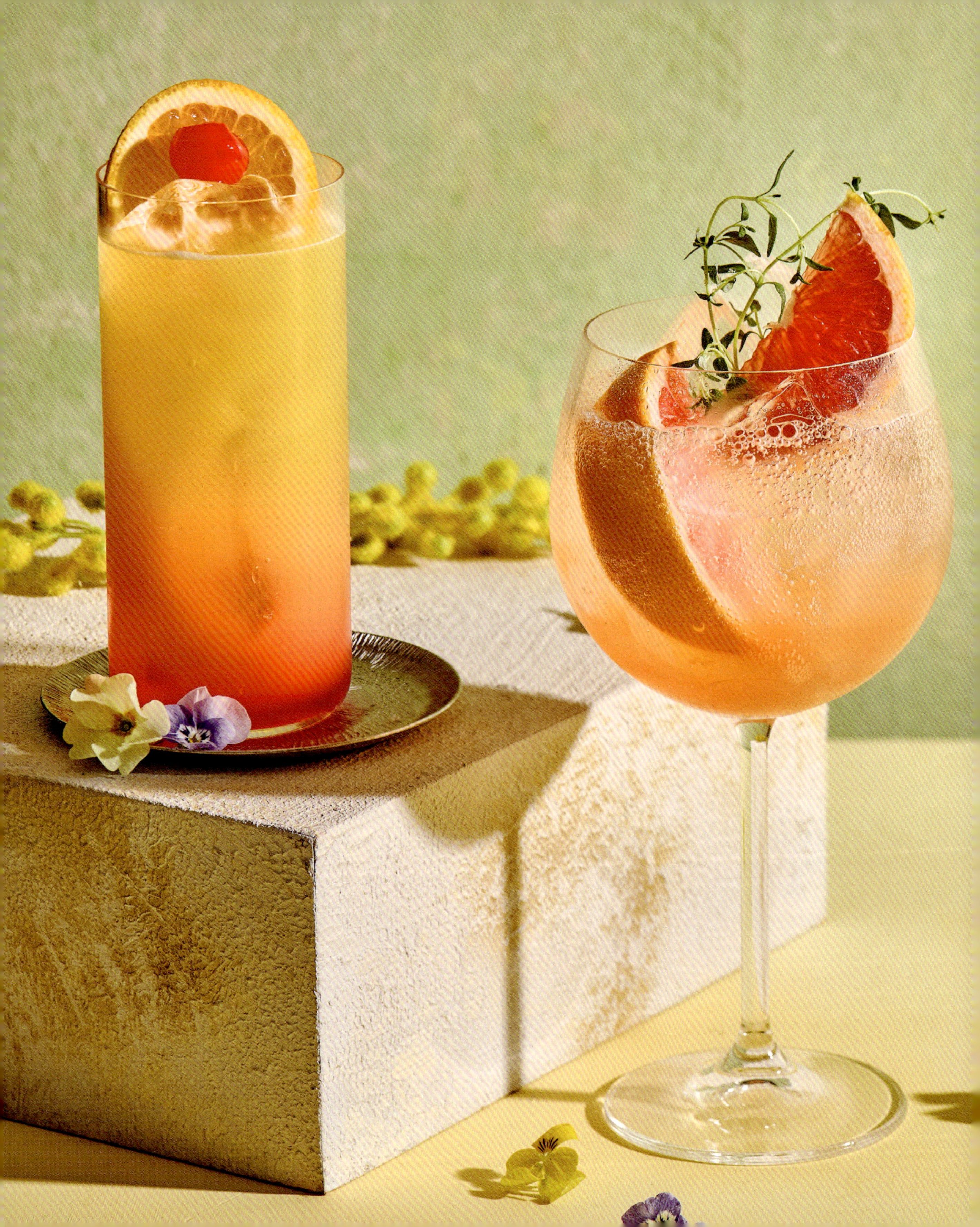

TROPICAL SUNRISE

Tequila can be used to create a host of delicious drinks, all of which are great inspiration for mocktails, such as this take on a Tequila Sunrise.

25 ml/¾ oz. Almave Blanco (optional; see Note)
50 ml/1¾ oz. pineapple juice
100 ml/3¾ oz. orange juice
1 teaspoon Saline Solution (see page 125)
2 teaspoons grenadine

SERVES 1

Shake the ingredients, except the grenadine, with ice and strain into a tall ice-filled glass. Slowly pour the grenadine down the side of the glass so that it sinks, creating the characteristic sunrise effect.

NOTE:
Almave Blanco is an non-alcoholic 'spirit' distilled from blue agave and a useful 0% abv substitute for tequila.

THE DOVE

A deliciously refreshing alternative to the popular Paloma cocktail.

50 ml/1¾ oz. freshly squeezed pink or ruby grapefruit juice
25 ml/¾ oz. Almave Blanco (see Note above)
2 teaspoons Simple Sugar Syrup (see page 123) or Vanilla Syrup (see page 124)
1 teaspoon Saline Solution (see page 125)
100 ml/3¾ oz. sparkling water
a sprig of thyme, grapefruit wedge and sea salt, to garnish

SERVES 1

Shake all of the ingredients except the sparkling water with ice, then strain into a large balloon glass filled with ice. Garnish with a sprig of thyme (optional), a wedge of grapefruit and a sprinkle of sea salt.

DAISY, DAISY

For fans of a Margarita, this drink offers the same lip-smacking hit of citrus and salt.

50 ml/1¾ oz. Almave Blanco (see Note, page 29)
25 ml/¾ oz. freshly squeezed lime juice
25 ml/¾ oz. agave syrup
1 teaspoon Saline Solution (see page 125)
3–4 dashes orange bitters (or squeeze 2 pieces of orange peel into the shaker)
Himalayan pink salt, to rim the glass
edible flowers, to garnish (optional)

SERVES 1

Salt the rim of a rocks glass (or decorate as shown), add ice and set aside.

Combine all of the ingredients in a cocktail shaker with ice. Shake vigorously and strain into the prepared glass. Garnish with edible flowers, if liked.

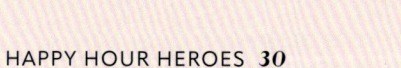

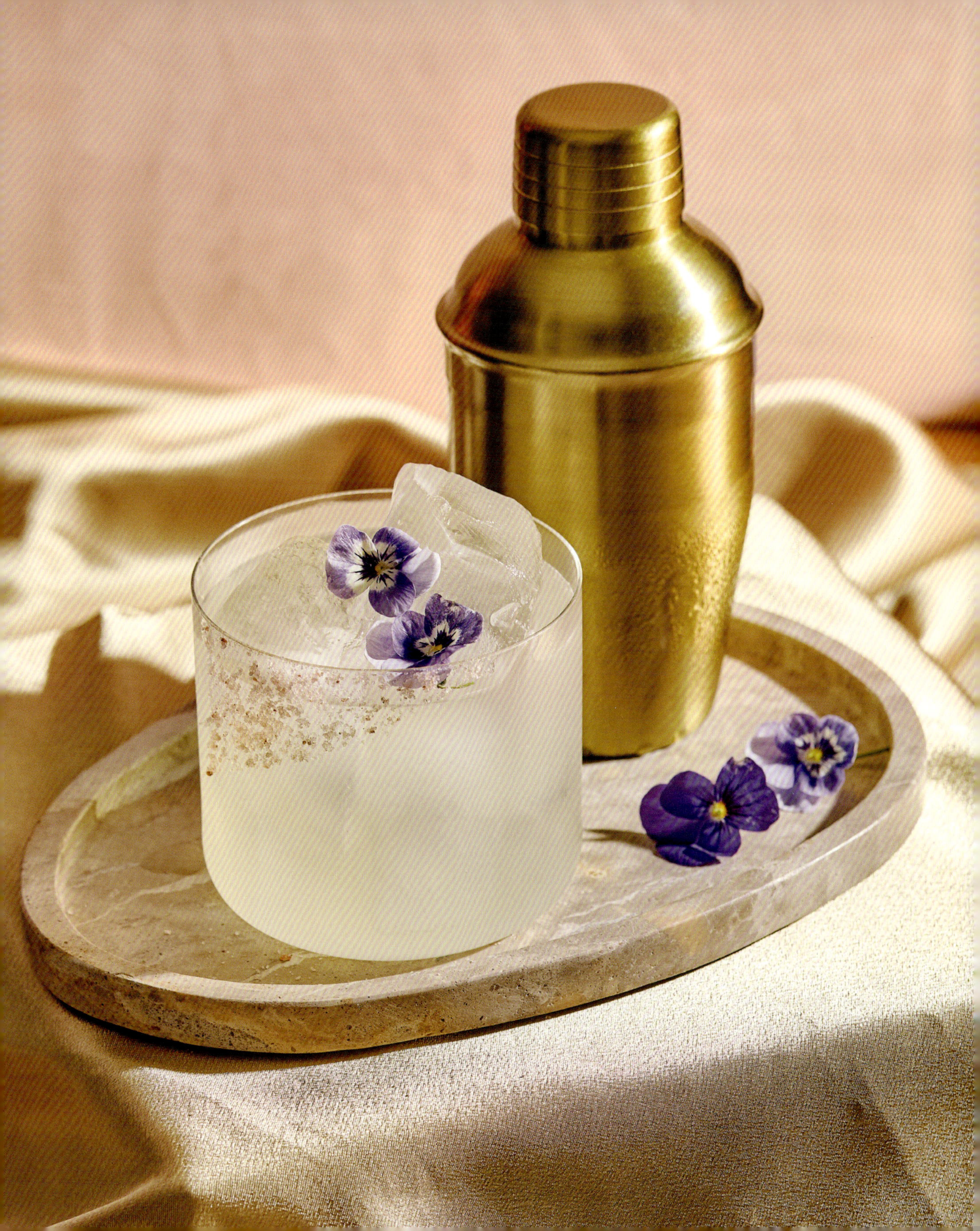

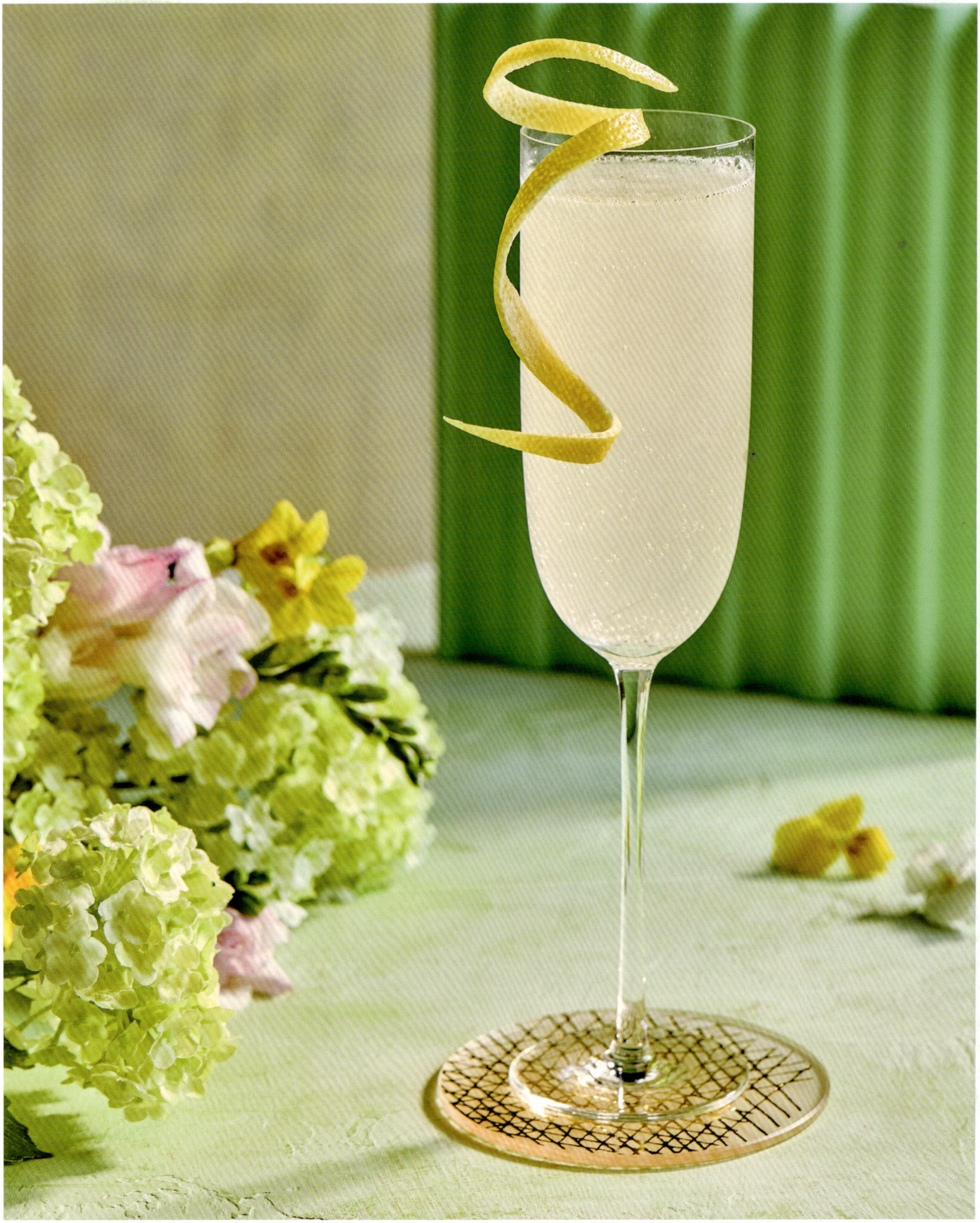

FRENCH 7.5

This take on a French 75, a drink named after a piece of artillery, may lack the power, but it's nonetheless of a delicious calibre.

30 ml/1 oz. freshly squeezed lemon juice
1 tablespoon icing/confectioners' sugar (using this type of sugar helps with texture and balance)
45 ml/1½ oz. gin substitute, such as Tanqueray 0.0%
100 ml/3¾ oz. non-alcoholic sparkling dry wine, such as Oddbird Sparkling Blanc De Blancs
lemon peel, to garnish

SERVES 1

Add the lemon juice and icing sugar to a shaker and stir to combine. Add the gin substitute and ice and shake. Strain into a flute glass and top up with the non-alcoholic wine. Stir gently and garnish with a long piece of lemon peel.

DUKE OF EARL

A quick and easy way to add some sparkle to iced tea, this is a great drink for festive or celebratory occasions.

50 ml/1¾ oz. Earl Grey tea, chilled (see Note below)
100 ml/3¾ oz. non-alcoholic sparkling wine
orange peel, to garnish

SERVES 1

Add the tea to a chilled champagne flute, followed by the wine. Garnish with a long, thin strip of orange peel.

NOTE:
If you're feeling adventurous, you can experiment with other teas, such as English breakfast or jasmine green.

COKE & RUM

The classic double act. Rum and coke has been a long-time staple at the bar and, thanks to some innovative new products, this non-alcoholic version can be a firm favourite, too.

1 teaspoon high-flavoured rum, such as Merser's Small Rum
100 ml/3¾ oz. cola
orange peel, to garnish (optional)

SERVES 1

Add the ingredients to an ice-filled glass. No garnish is strictly necessary, but, if desired, orange peel typically works better than lemon.

TONIC & GIN

Thankfully, for fans of a G&T, there are lots of options to create low- or no-alcohol versions of this classic drink.

50 ml/1¾ oz. low-alcohol gin substitute, such as Hayman's London Light or Warner's Juniper Double Dry
150 ml/5¼ oz. tonic water, or to taste
lemon wheels, to garnish

SERVES 1

Combine the ingredients in an ice-filled glass, or follow your individual product's instructions. Garnish with a few wheels of lemon.

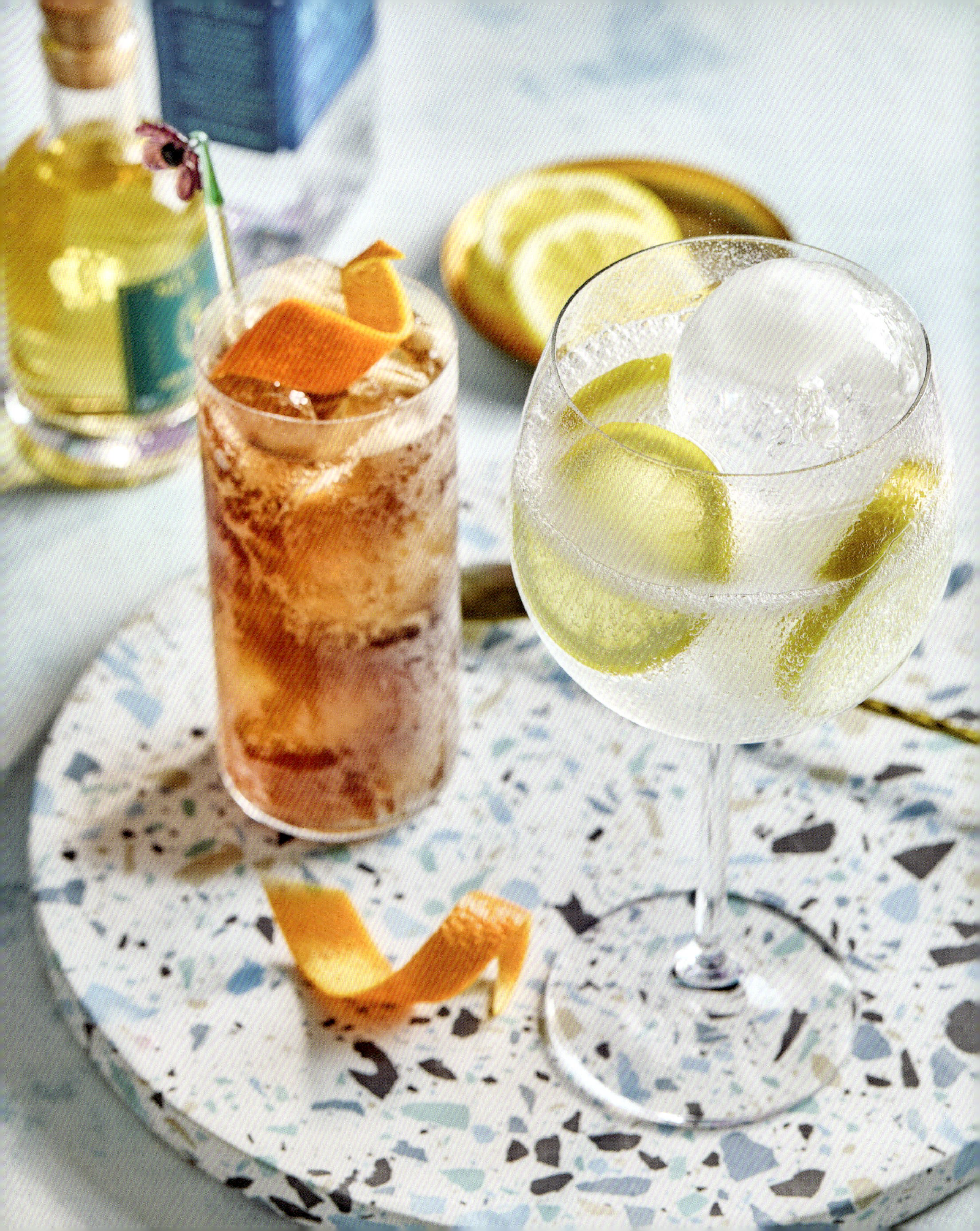

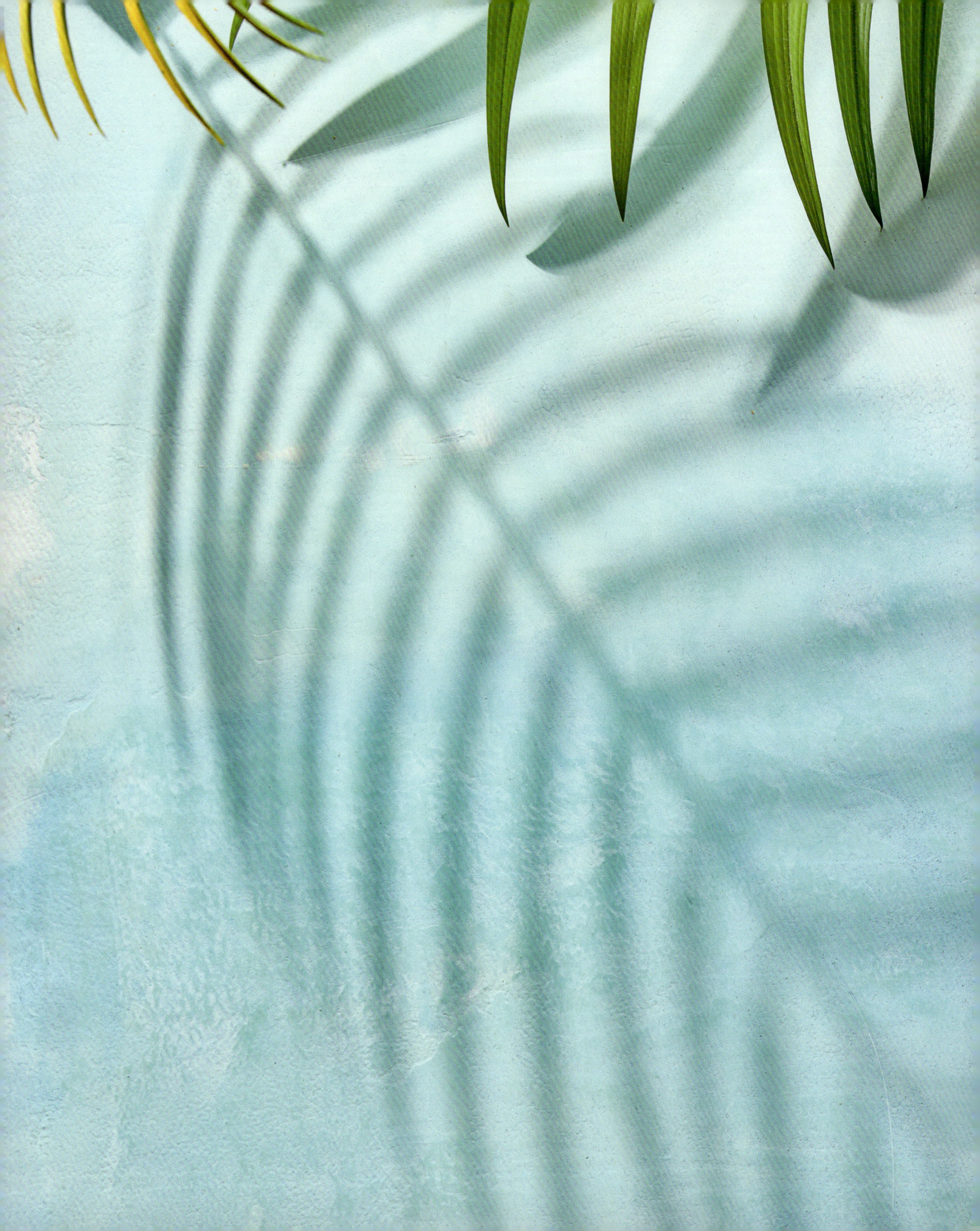

TROPICAL TREATS

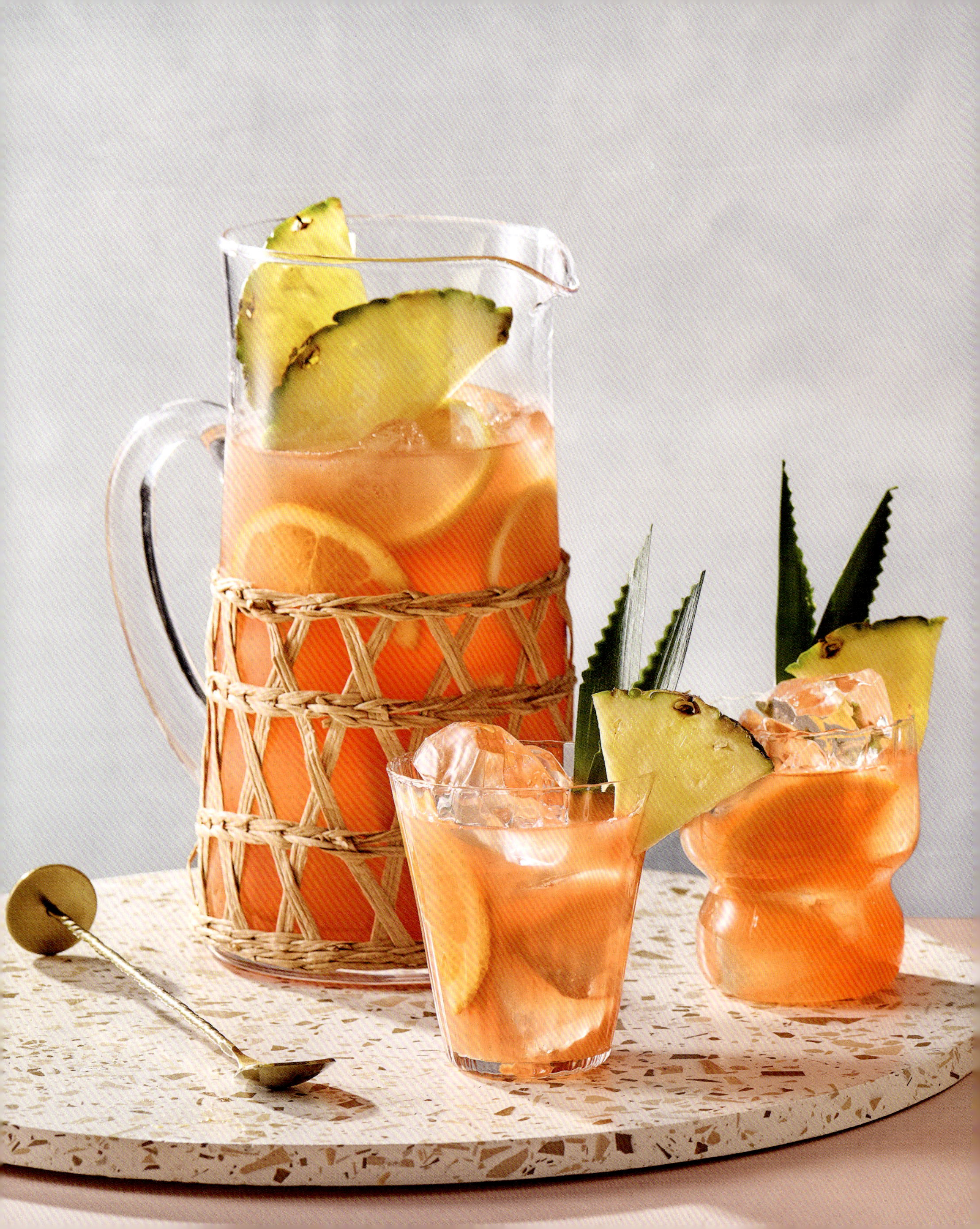

FRUIT PUNCH

A classic US soft drink that often comes in powdered forms, such as Kool-Aid and Crystal Light. This is a delicious recipe for a fresh version.

200 ml/7 oz. fresh pineapple Juice
150 ml/5¼ oz. unsweetened apple juice
150 ml/5¼ oz. passion fruit juice drink (such as Rubicon)
100 ml/3¾ oz. freshly squeezed orange juice
50 ml/1¾ oz. cherry juice, or 30 ml/1 oz. Cherry Syrup (see page 78)
50 ml/1¾ oz. freshly squeezed lime Juice
100 ml/3¾ oz. still mineral water, chilled (optional)

TO GARNISH
1 orange, sliced into wheels
4 pineapple wedges
pineapple leaves (optional)

SERVES 4

Combine all of the ingredients in a jug/pitcher and stir gently to combine. Add the orange slices and chill until ready to serve. Fill four highball glasses with ice cubes and slowly pour the mix into them. Garnish each glass with some of the orange slices, a pineapple wedge and a pineapple leaf (if using). Serve at once.

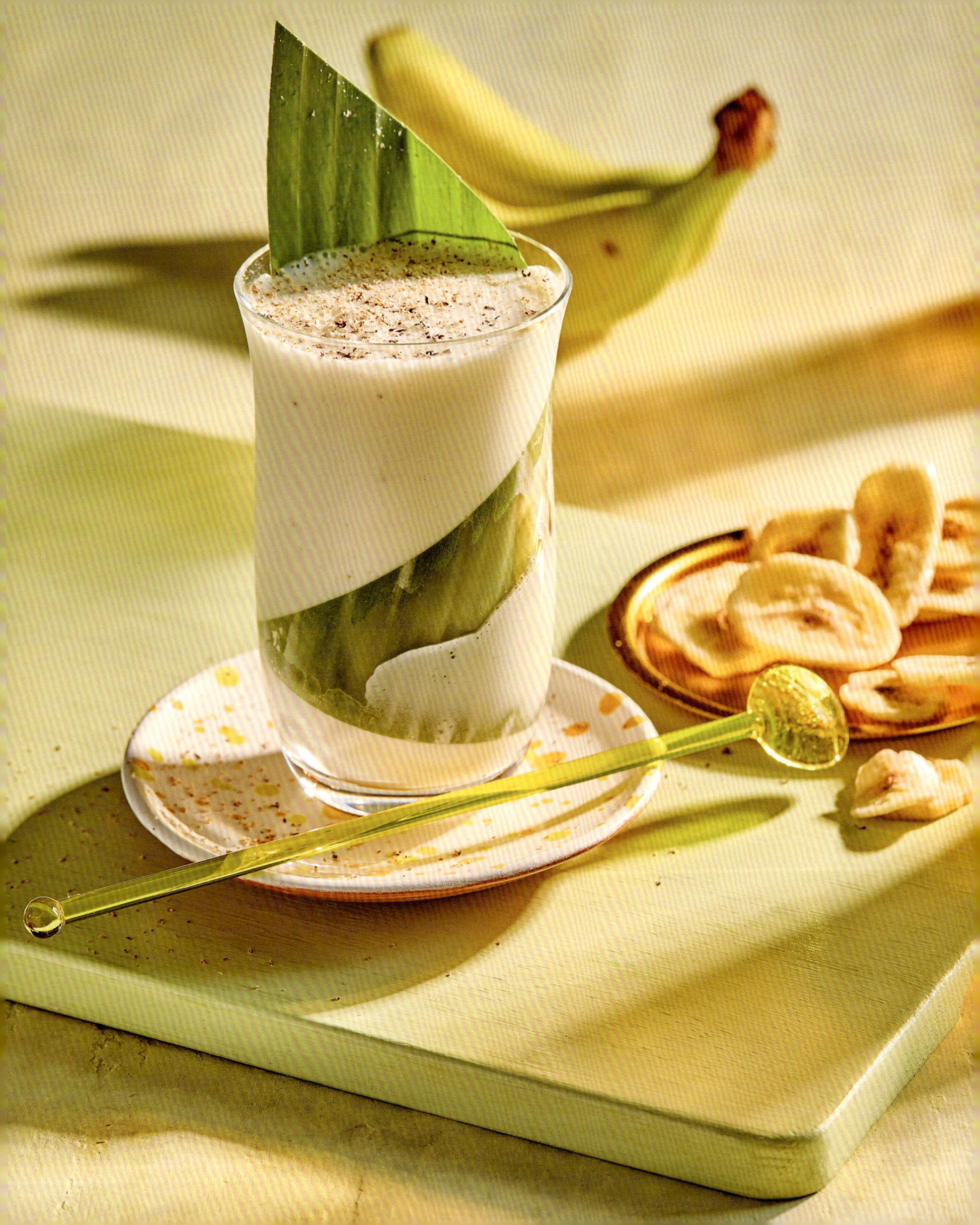

BANANA BATIDA

This milky drink is popular in Latin America, in particular Brazil. Batida means 'to beat or churn' in Portuguese and so the drink is usually shaken or blended. Occasionally, it is based on fruit juice.

120 ml/½ cup banana jam/preserve (or 1 ripe banana)
100 ml/3¾ oz. sweetened condensed milk
50 ml/1¾ oz. unsweetened coconut milk (if using canned, use full-fat and shake it up before use)
20 ml/¾ oz. freshly squeezed lime juice
'wet' (slightly melted) ice
banana leaf and grated nutmeg, to garnish

SERVES 1

Add all the ingredients to a blender and blend on medium speed until mixed. Pour into a glass and garnish with a banana leaf and freshly grated nutmeg.

NOTE:
For a less thick version scoop the cream off the top of the canned coconut milk (or use cartoned coconut milk) and use 30 ml/1 oz. lime juice and add 20 ml/¾ oz. Simple Sugar Syrup (see page 123), too.

PEANUT BUTTER BANANA BATIDA

Peanut butter and banana is said to have been Elvis' favourite sandwich filling, so here's a drink variation fit for The King.

120 ml/½ cup banana jam (or 1 ripe banana)
3 tablespoons creamy peanut butter (no need to get fancy here, but make sure that it's salted)
45 ml/1½ oz. sweetened condensed milk
180 ml/6 oz. unsweetened coconut milk (if using canned, use full-fat and shake it up before use)
30 ml/1 oz. freshly squeezed lime Juice
30 ml/1 oz. Simple Sugar Syrup (see page 123)
pinch of sea salt (kosher salt)
'wet' (slightly melted) ice
ground sweet cinnamon, to garnish

SERVES 1

Add all the ingredients to a blender and blend on medium speed until mixed. Pour into a glass and garnish with a pinch of ground sweet cinnamon.

TROPICAL TREATS

ISLAND-STYLE ICED TEAS

On the face of it, ice or iced tea couldn't be simpler: brew black tea and then add ice. It is often credited with being invented at the 1904 World Fair in St Louis, Missouri, an event that certainly helped to spread its popularity.

There are three main ways to make iced tea:
1. Brew it hot and then cool it immediately with ice (be careful when doing this, as the temperature change can often shatter a glass or ceramic container).
2. Brew it hot and allow it to cool.
3. Brew the tea cold from the start (this will take longer).

TO A SAUCEPAN ADD:
2–3 black tea bags of your choice
500 ml/17 oz. boiling water (from a kettle)

Each method has its pros and cons in terms of time, convenience and taste, but no way is definitively right or wrong; it's down to personal preference.

Allow to brew for 3–5 minutes (or as per instructions) and then remove the teabags and carefully add ice.

The type of tea used is also a personal choice. Some swear by Lipton's Orange Pekoe, which is citrusy, similar to Ceylon tea, and is complemented by a squeeze of lemon. Assam tea is bold, rich and malty and works well with the powerful zing of lime, whilst Earl Grey has a refined floral, citrus note from the bergamot. If in doubt, a classic English breakfast tea works well with most garnishes.

Sweetness level is another personal preference. Some prefer their tea unsweetened, perhaps with a squeeze of lemon, whilst others like a little sugar (and some like a lot!). Using a Simple Sugar Syrup (see page 123) to sweeten helps the sugar to dissolve into the mixture and gives you more control over the sweetness level. A rough gauge would be to use 2–20ml (a splash–½ oz) of Simple Sugar Syrup per 100 ml/3¾ oz. of unsweetened tea.

TROPICAL ICED TEA

300 ml/10½ oz. black tea, brewed
60 ml/2 oz. off-the-shelf pineapple syrup
90 ml/3 oz. fresh orange juice
pineapple chunks and orange wheels, to garnish

SERVES 1

Mix in a tall glass with ice. Garnish with pineapple chunks and orange wheels.

WATERMELON ICED TEA

200 ml/7 oz. black tea, brewed
60–90 ml/2–3 oz. Watermelon Purée (see below)
mint sprig, to garnish

SERVES 1

Fill a tall glass with ice, add the tea and watermelon and mix. Garnish with a mint sprig.

WATERMELON PURÉE
900 g/6 cups watermelon chunks
pinch of salt

In batches, purée the watermelon in a blender until smooth, adding little bits of water as needed (not too much to make the purée too runny). Add a pinch of salt.

TROPICAL TREATS

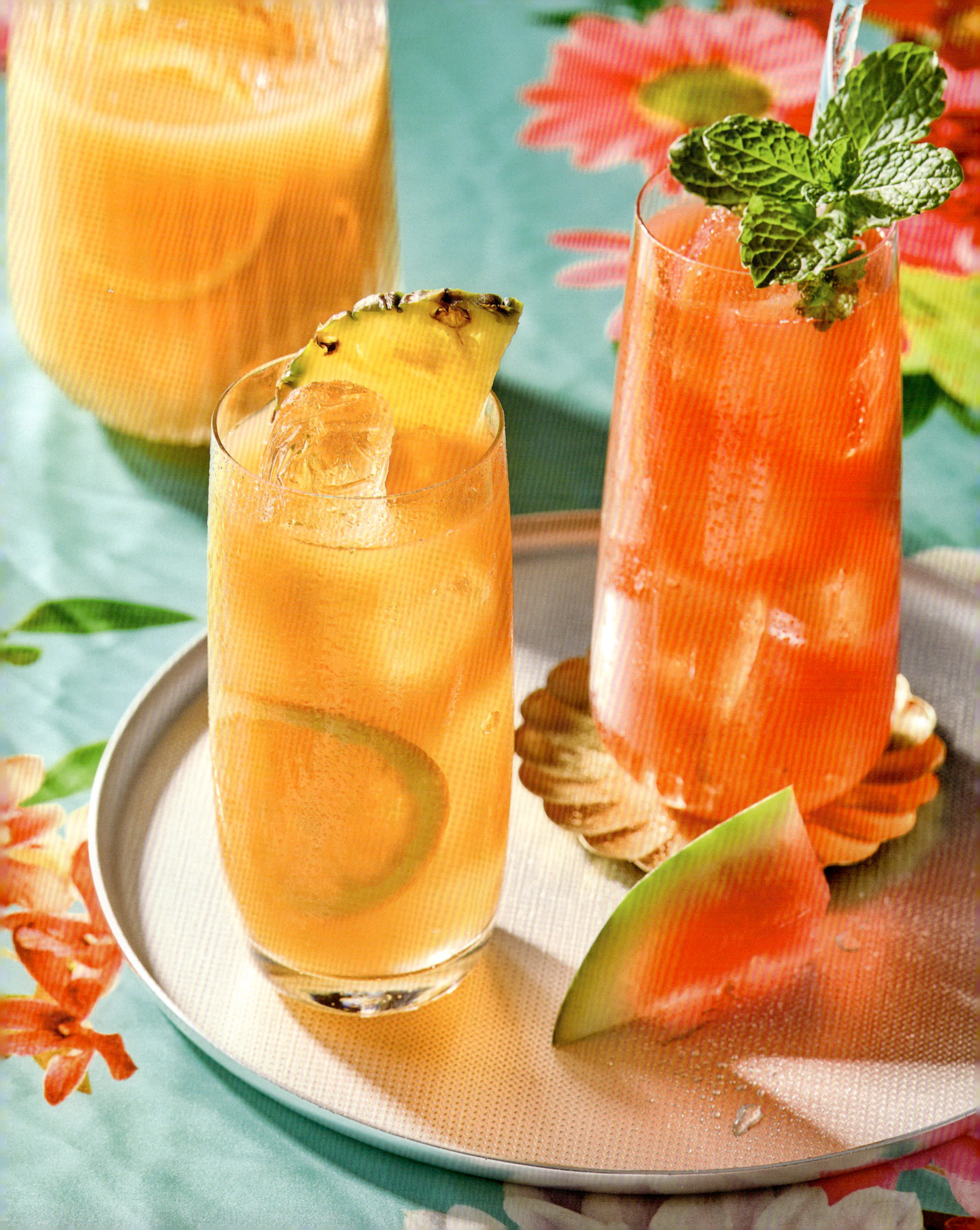

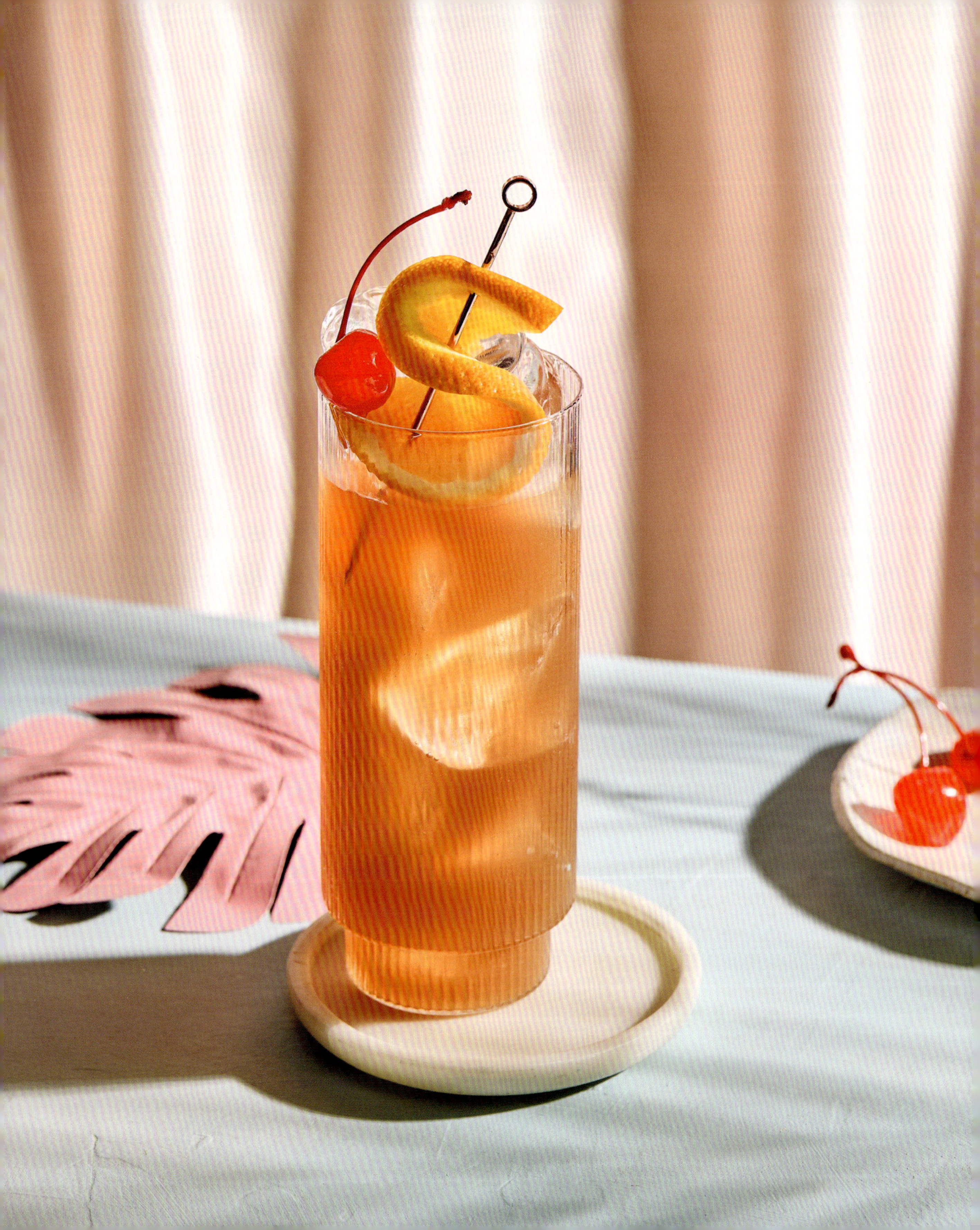

TEA BY THE SEA

Perfect for sipping by the pool on a hot, sunny day. This drink takes the key flavours of the classic summer cocktail Sex on the Beach – peach, orange and cranberry – and combines them in a refreshing drink.

100 ml/3¾ oz. peach iced tea
50 ml/1¾ oz. orange juice
50 ml/1¾ oz. cranberry juice
orange wheel and cocktail cherry for garnish

Shake the ingredients vigorously with ice and strain into a tall ice-filled glass. Garnish with a wheel of orange and a cocktail cherry.

SERVES

MANGO TANGO

A simple, but refreshing drink with mango, which provides a luscious fruitiness, and lime, giving it a lively zing.

60 ml/2 oz. mango juice or nectar
15 ml/½ oz. freshly squeezed lime juice
15 ml/½ oz. Simple Sugar Syrup (see page 123)
3 dashes angostura bitters
lime wheel and mint leaf, to garnish

SERVES 1

Add the ingredients to a shaker and shake with ice. Strain into a coupe glass and garnish with a lime wheel and mint leaf.

TROPICAL TREATS 47

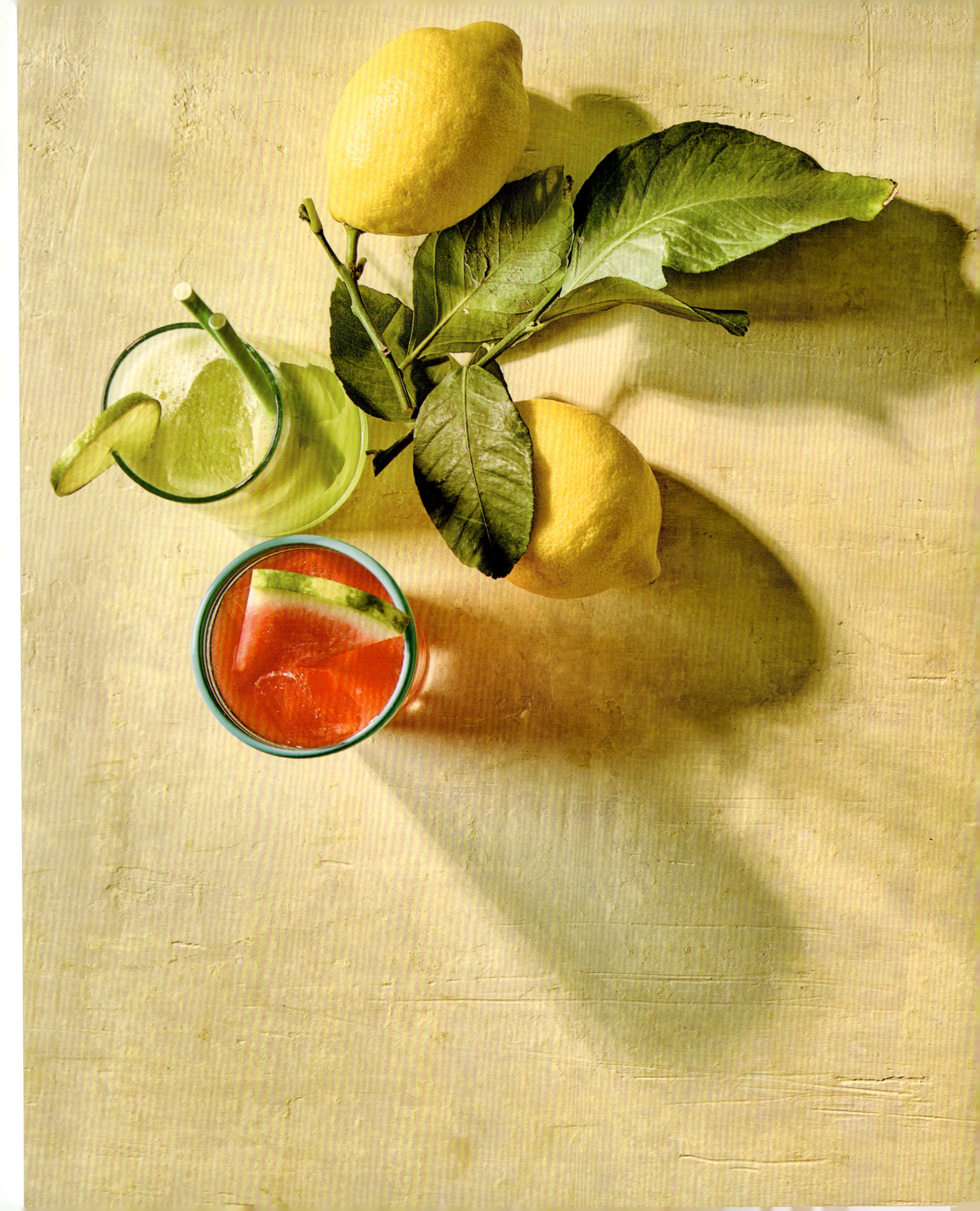

PORCH DRINKS

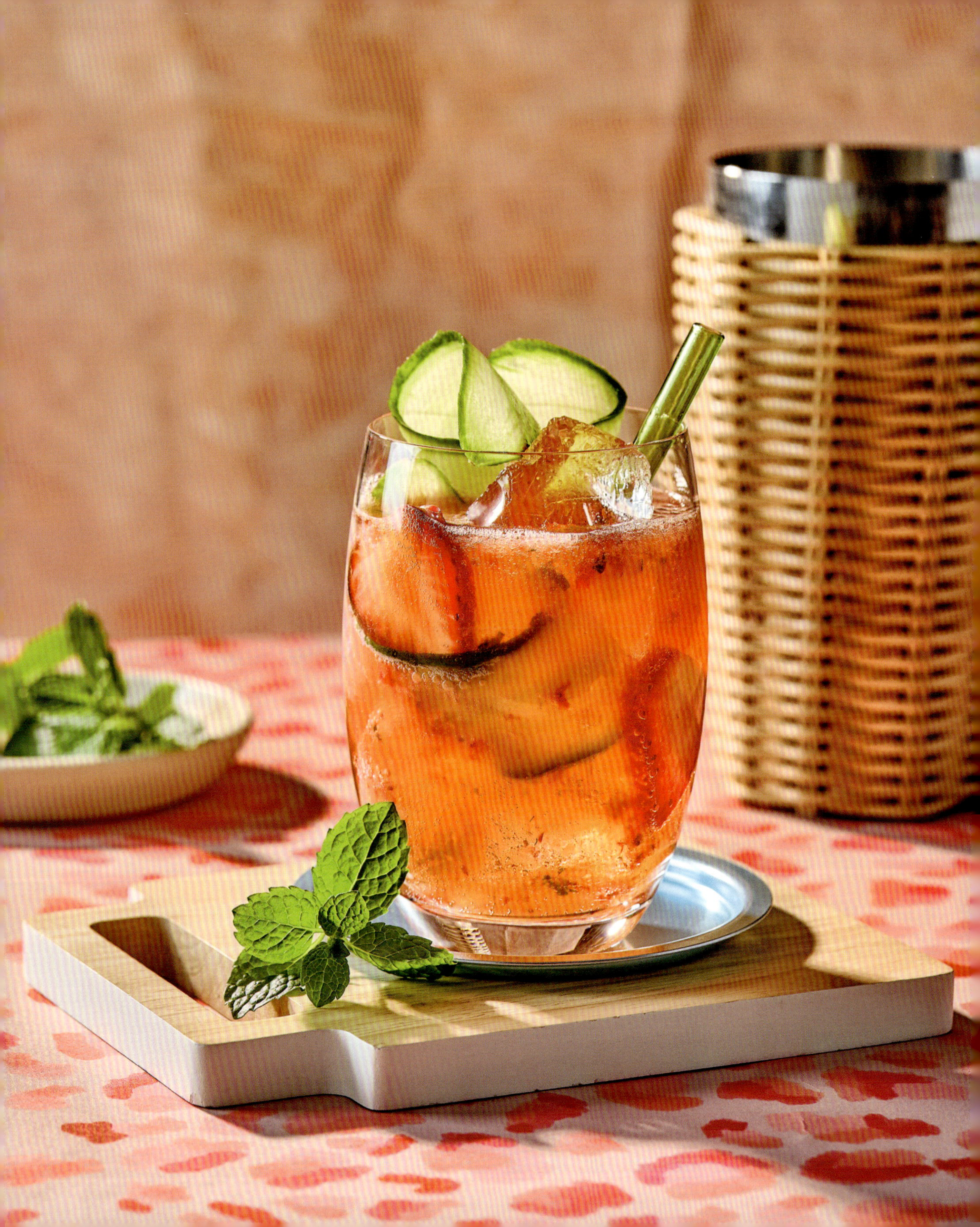

COTTAGE GARDEN CUP

Picnics, garden parties, Wimbledon; if it's the summer in the UK, there is one quintessential drink: the Fruit or Summer Cup. The most popular brand of which is, of course, Pimm's.
Any fan of a fruit cup will tell you that presentation is key and that is the case here: a stylish, elegant glass and fresh, vibrant ingredients and garnishes are critical for success.

4–6 medium strawberries, plus extra to garnish

3 tablespoons cubed cucumber, plus extra to garnish

6–8 mint leaves, plus extra to garnish

50 ml/1¾ oz. Ginger Syrup (see page 124) or Simple Sugar Syrup (see page 123)

200 ml/7 oz. cold-brew black tea (or other black tea brewed and cooled to room temperature)

500 ml/17 oz. ginger beer (or use bitter lemon tonic or sparkling lemonade for a lighter version)

SERVES 4

In a shaker, add the strawberries, cucumber, mint leaves and syrup, and muddle. Add the tea and some ice and shake. Dirty dump (including the ice shards) into a glass jug/pitcher and top up with fresh ice. Fill with ginger beer and stir to mix.

To serve, pour into individual ice-filled glasses and garnish with thin cucumber wheels or ribbons, slices of strawberries and mint sprigs.

NOTE:

For additional botanical complexity you can add fresh herbs like tarragon, parsley, thyme or even spicy rocket/arugula. For a more savoury route, substitute the strawberry slices for garden-fresh tomatoes, watermelon, basil and a pinch of salt, before adding a splash of apple cider vinegar and using soda water/selzer instead of the ginger beer.

PORCH DRINKS

AGUA DE SANDÍA & AGUA FRESCA

Translated from the Spanish as 'fresh water', these drinks are a combination of water, sugar and a variety of fruits, often complemented with other flavours from grains, flowers or leaves. They are typically made in large batches and served throughout the day – they are designed to be light and refreshing.

AGUA DE SANDÍA
(WATERMELON AGUA FRESCA)

120 ml/4 oz. Watermelon Purée (see page 44)
60 ml/2 oz. filtered water, chilled, or as needed
15 ml/½ oz. freshly squeezed lime juice
15 ml/½ oz. Simple Sugar Syrup (see page 123), or to taste
sea salt (kosher salt), to taste
watermelon wedges, to garnish

SERVES 1

Mix the watermelon purée, filtered water, lime juice and syrup together. Add more water if the purée is too thick. Pour into a jug/pitcher and adjust to taste for sweetness and salt.

AGUA FRESCA DE PEPINO
(CUCUMBER LIMEADE AGUA FRESCA)

3 cucumbers, peeled, seeded and cubed
100 ml/3¾ oz. freshly squeezed lime juice
50 ml/1¾ oz. Simple Sugar Syrup (see page 123), or to taste
1.2 litres/quarts filtered water, chilled, or as needed
sea salt (kosher salt), to taste
lime wheels, to garnish

SERVES 2–4

Blend the cucumbers, lime juice and syrup together with 200 ml/7 oz. of the filtered water until smooth. Pour into a jug/pitcher (straining if you want to remove the pulp) and add the remaining water, before adjusting to taste for sweetness and salt. Pour into glasses and garnish with lime wheels.

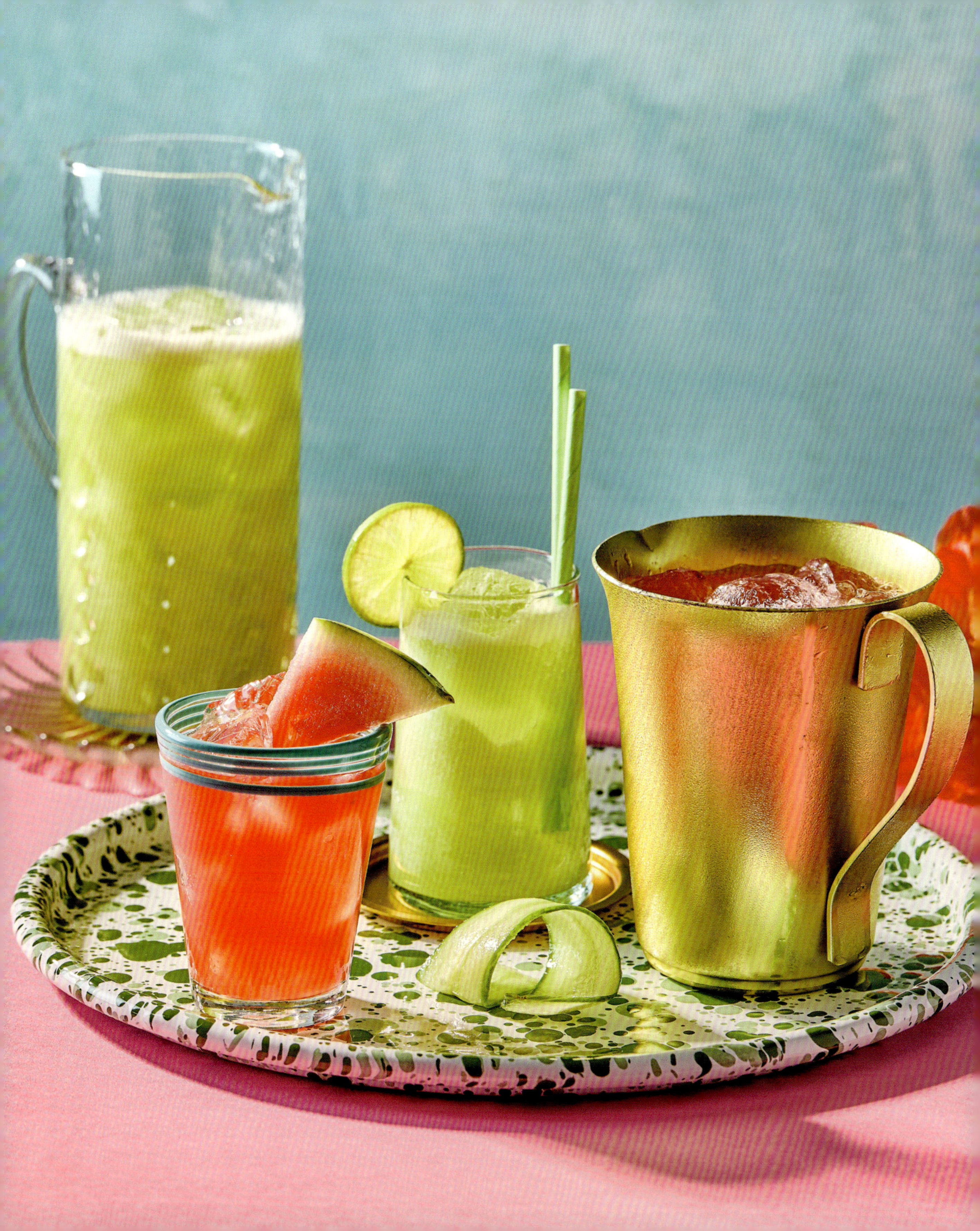

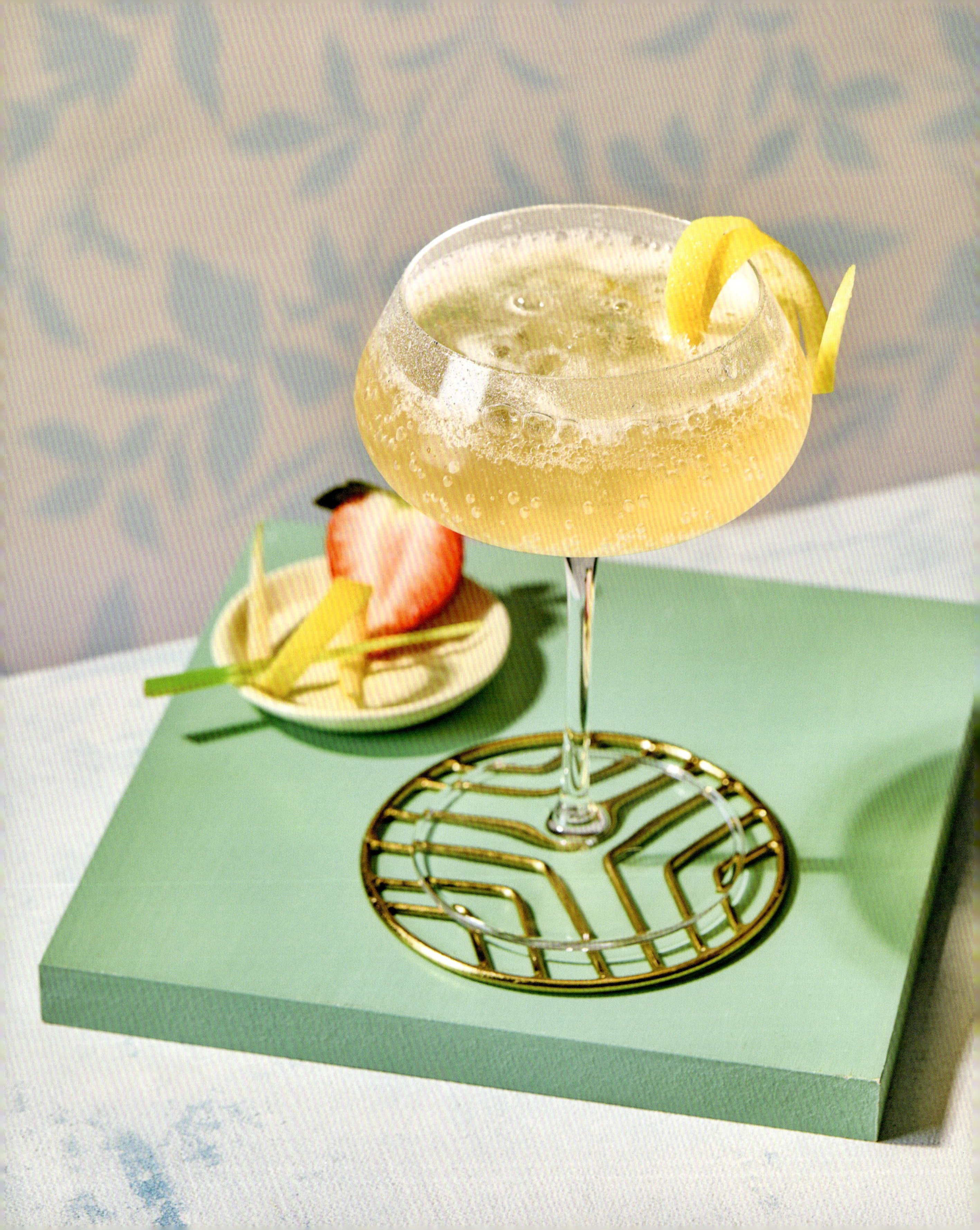

PRESBYTERIAN

The classic British highball, but without the blended Scotch whisky. At least a century old, the exact origins of this drink are lost to the sands of time, although the name is likely a reference to the Christian denomination that has its roots in Scotland.

Ginger ale differs from ginger beer in a few ways. Ginger beer is often cloudy and has a more fiery ginger flavour; it is often made at least in part by fermentation. Ginger ale is clearer and less intense. Dry ginger ale is even lighter and has less sweetness. Schweppes Canada Dry is an example of a dry ginger ale.

75 ml/2½ oz. soda water, chilled
75 ml/2½ oz. ginger ale, chilled (such as Fever-Tree)
lemon peel or strawberry slice, to garnish

SERVES 1

Add the soda water and ginger ale to a chilled coupe glass and garnish with lemon peel or a slice of strawberry. Serve without ice. For a longer drink, increase the quantity of each soda to 100 ml/3¾ oz. and serve over ice in a tumbler.

VARIATION:

Stop the Presses is a crisper, more tart drink. To make it, substitute the soda water with still lemonade (homemade, see page 58, is particularly delicious). Serve in a large, ice-filled balloon glass and garnish with a lemon wedge.

LEMONADE STAND

When life gives you lemons... For many people, lemonade production is one of their first forays into the tough realities of catering, business and small-scale manufacturing, whether as an actual curbside enterprise or just for fun at home.

LEMONADE

150 ml/5¼ oz. freshly squeezed lemon juice
400 ml/14 oz. filtered water, chilled
75 ml/2½ oz. Simple Sugar Syrup (see page 123), or to taste
citrus wheels, to garnish

SERVES 2–3

Add all of the ingredients to a jug/pitcher and stir. When ready to serve, add plenty of ice and stir again. Serve in small tumblers with a garnish of citrus wheels.

VARIATIONS: (Follow the lemonade method, above)

LIMEADE

100 ml/3½ oz. freshly squeezed lime juice
200 ml/7 oz. filtered water, chilled
50 ml/1¾ oz. Simple Sugar Syrup (see page 123), or to taste

CHERRYADE

100 ml/3½ oz. freshly squeezed lemon juice
200 ml/7 oz. water, chilled
50 ml/1¾ oz. Cherry Syrup (see page 78), or to taste

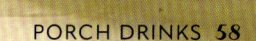

PORCH DRINKS

ORANGEADE

75 ml/2½ oz. freshly squeezed orange juice
25 ml/¾ oz. freshly squeezed lemon juice
200 ml/7 oz. filtered water, chilled
25 ml/¾ oz. Simple Sugar Syrup (see page 123), or to taste

HIBISCUS LEMONADE

Follow the lemonade recipe (left), but infuse the filtered water with hibiscus tea bags before use.

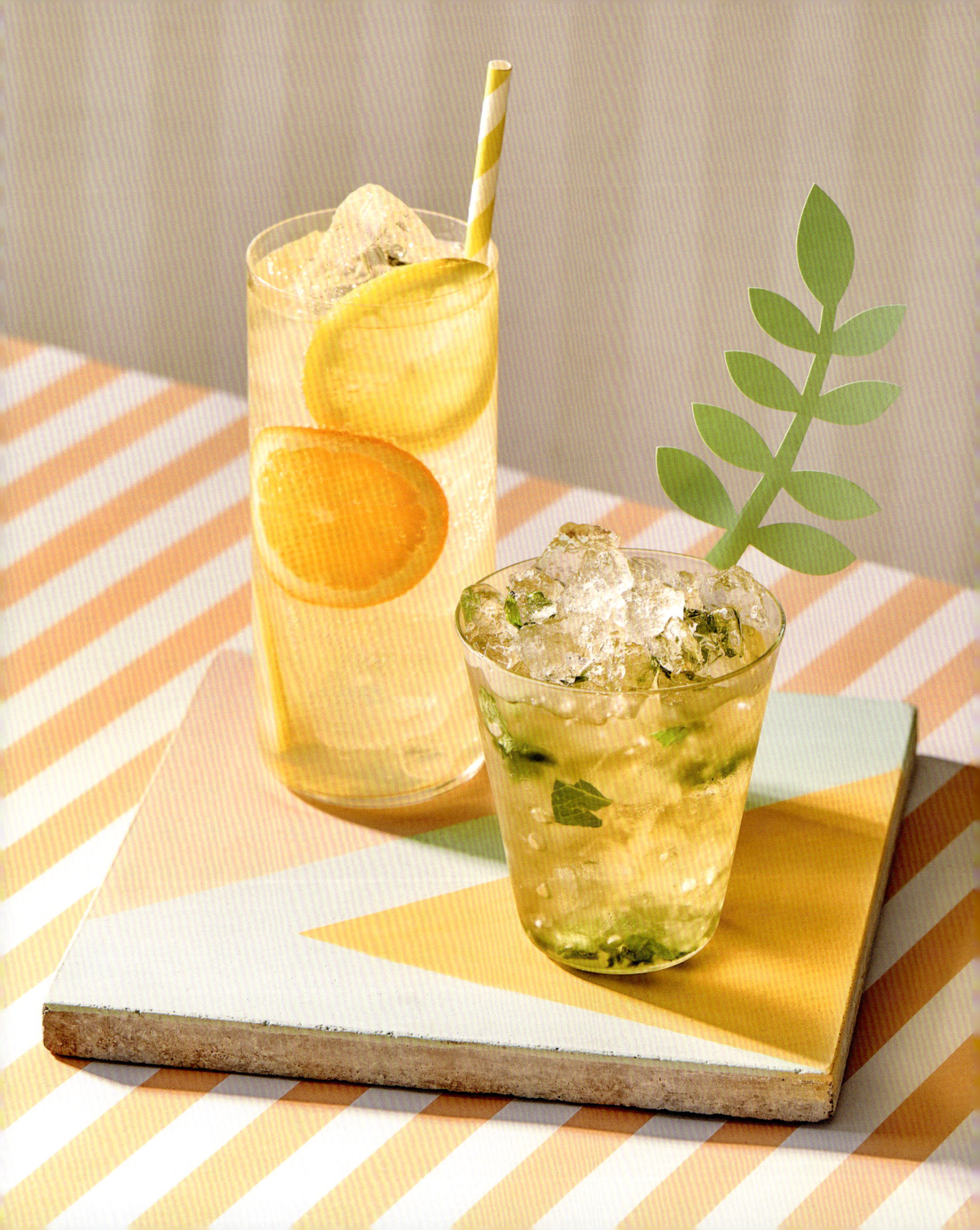

CHAMOMILE COLLINS

Whilst not technically 'tea' (i.e. not made from a tea plant), there are a variety of fruit, floral and herbal infusions that make great bases for modern mocktails.

15 ml/½ oz. freshly squeezed lemon juice
15 ml/½ oz. Simple Sugar Syrup (see page 123)
150 ml/5¼ oz. chamomile tea, chilled
50 ml/1¾ oz. soda water
orange and lemon wheels, to garnish

SERVES 1

Add the ingredients to a tall, ice-filled glass and stir. Top up with the soda water. Garnish with orange and lemon wheels and add a straw.

COOL MINT FRAPPÉ

Mint leaves contain menthol and eucalyptol, which both have a natural cooling effect. When chilled and combined with ice, mint tea is one of the ultimate thirst quenchers.

leaves from 1 mint sprig
250 ml/9 oz. mint tea, chilled
15 ml/½ oz. Simple Sugar Syrup (see page 123; optional)
2–3 dashes chocolate bitters (optional)

SERVES 1

Crush a few mint leaves in the base of a tumbler. Add crushed ice and the rest of the ingredients. Stir gently.

GRAPEFRUIT RADLER

A mix of beer and soda or juice similar to the British 'shandy' or French 'panaché'. Radler is German for 'cyclist' and this variation was first mixed in June 1922 at the Kugler Alm Tavern in Munich by Franz Kugler. Inundated by an approximate 23,000 cyclists that day, he was worried about running out of beer and so cut it with a lemon soda. Today, radlers are available around the world and are made using a wide variety of different citrus soda and juices.

salt, for rimming the glass, as pictured
30 ml/1 oz. 0% gin, brand of your choice (optional)
35 ml/1 oz. grapefruit juice
15 ml/½ oz. freshly squeezed lemon juice
15 ml/½ oz. Simple Sugar Syrup (see page 123)
35 ml/1 oz. soda water or grapefruit seltzer water
300 ml/10½ oz. non-alcoholic lager (typically 0.05–0.5% ABV)
grapefruit wedge, to garnish

Salt the rim of a rocks glass. Add the gin (if using), grapefruit juice, lemon juice, syrup and soda water to a chilled glass and mix. Add the non-alcoholic beer (and ice cubes if you are porch drinking) and garnish with a grapefruit or lemon wedge.

SERVES 1

SPEZI

This combination of cola and orange originated in Germany in the 1950s. The name is a contraction of 'spezial-cola-misch' (special cola mix) and it is a popular soft drink in Germany. Spezi is one particular brand; Coca-Cola has their own version, named Mezzo Mix. Today, it is widely available across Germany, Austria and Switzerland, but it is easy to make your own.

240 ml/8½ oz. Orange Fanta (or use Lemon Fanta to create a Lemon Spezi)
240 ml/8½ oz. cola
lemon and orange wedges, to garnish

Combine the sodas in a well-iced pint glass and add the garnish.

SERVES 1

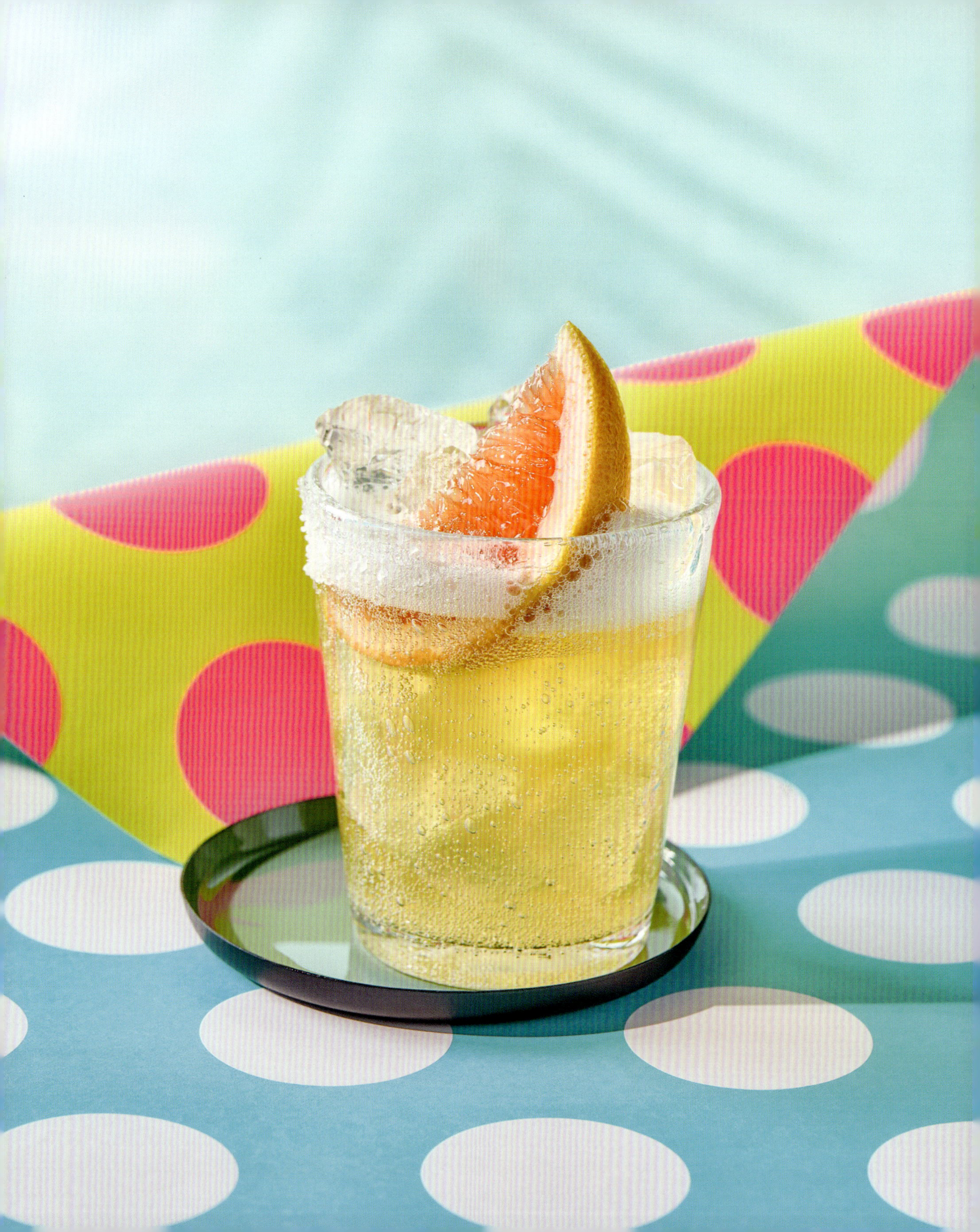

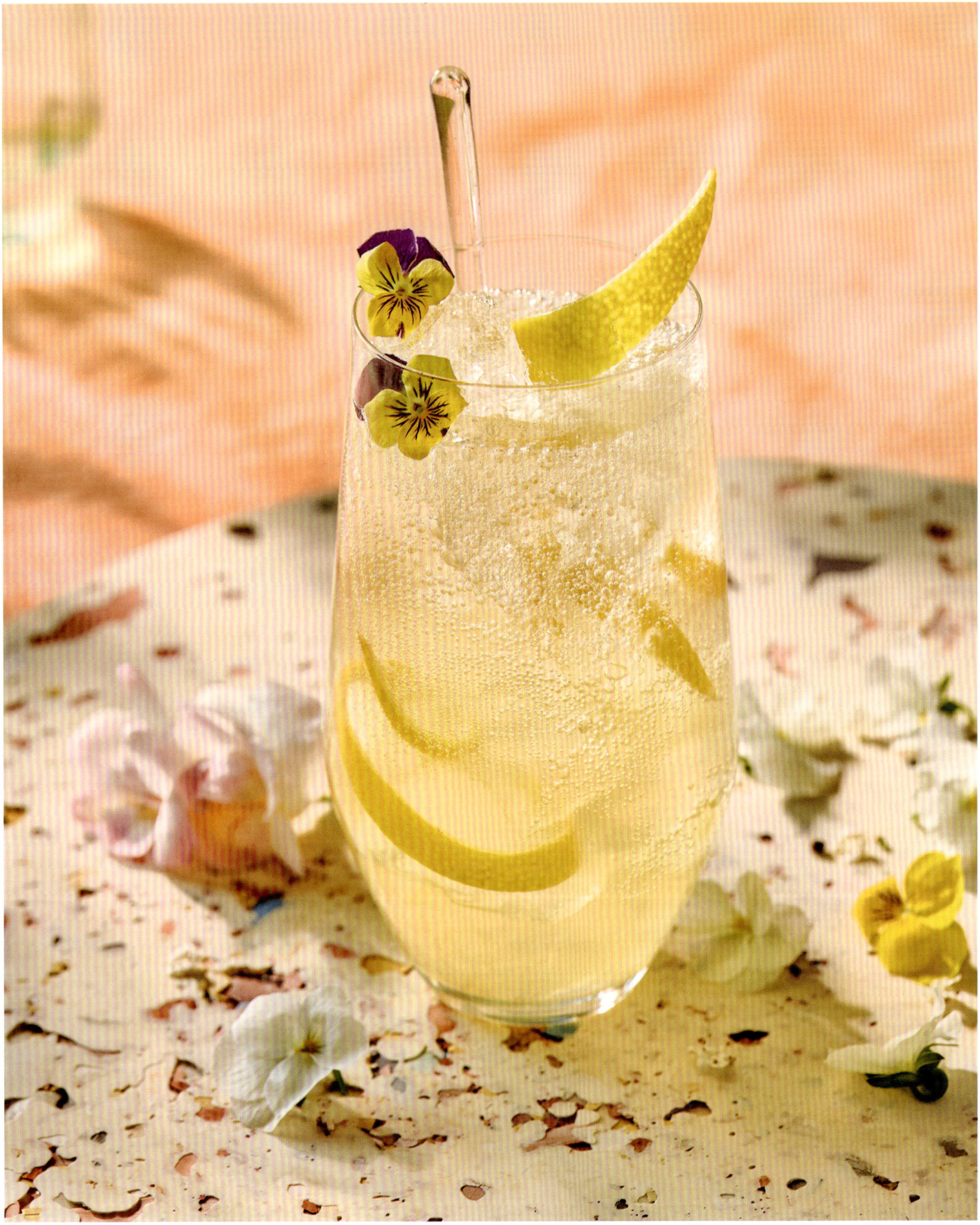

EASY BEING GREEN

Tea can form a great base for various drinks. Instructions for making iced tea can be found on page 44. Green tea, unlike black tea, has not been subject to the processes of wilting and oxidation; this results in a tea with a more fresh, grassy, even floral quality.

50 ml/1¾ oz. green tea, chilled
15 ml/½ oz. freshly squeezed lemon juice
10–15 ml/⅓–½ oz. Simple Sugar Syrup (see page 123; optional)
soda water, to top up
lemon peel and edible flowers, to garnish

SERVES 1

Add the ingredients to a tall, well-iced glass and stir. Top up with soda water and garnish with edible flowers and lemon peel.

BIG T TIME

An unusual combination on the face of it, but the result has the perfect balance of complexity and refreshment.

50 ml/1¾ oz. black tea, chilled
25 ml/¾ oz. orange juice
100 ml/3¾ oz. non-alcoholic lager (for example Asahi)
citrus wheels, to garnish

SERVES 1

Add the ingredients to a large, well-iced, stemmed balloon glass and garnish with a trio of citrus wheels.

PORCH DRINKS

BITTERS & SODA 3 WAYS

Cocktail bitters (sometimes referred to as non-potable bitters) usually come in small bottles with a dasher or a pipette. They have an intense, concentrated flavour and are not intended to be consumed on their own. They do, however, make a great seasoning for soft drinks, as only a few drops are used and the ABV of the drink stays well below 0.5% ABV.

ANGOSTURA BITTERS & TONIC

150 ml/5¼ oz. tonic water
3–4 dashes angostura bitters
lemon and lime wedges, to garnish

SERVES 1

Add the tonic to a chilled, ice-filled glass and add your dashes of the bitters. Garnish with a wedge of lemon and lime.

ORANGE BITTERS & COLA

150 ml/5¼ oz. cola
1 teaspoon Vanilla Syrup (see page 124)
3–4 dashes orange bitters
orange peel, to garnish

SERVES 1

Add the cola to a chilled, ice-filled glass and then add the syrup and bitters. Garnish with a long length of orange peel.

CHOCOLATE BITTERS & LEMON-LIME SODA

150 ml/5¼ oz. lemon-lime soda (e.g. 7Up or Sprite)
3–4 dashes chocolate bitters
pink grapefruit wedge, to garnish

SERVES 1

Add the soda to a chilled, ice-filled glass and dash in the bitters. Garnish with a wedge of pink grapefruit.

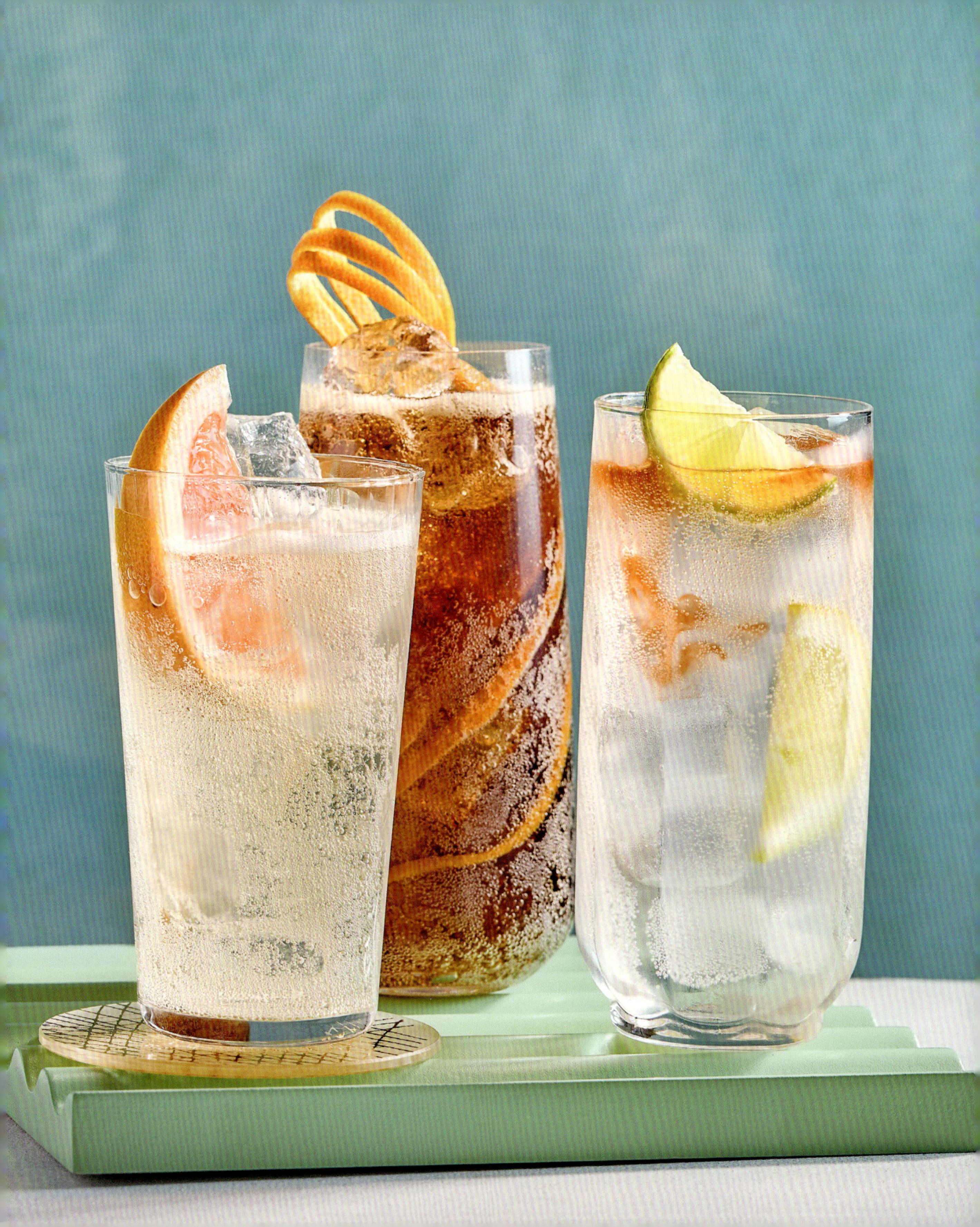

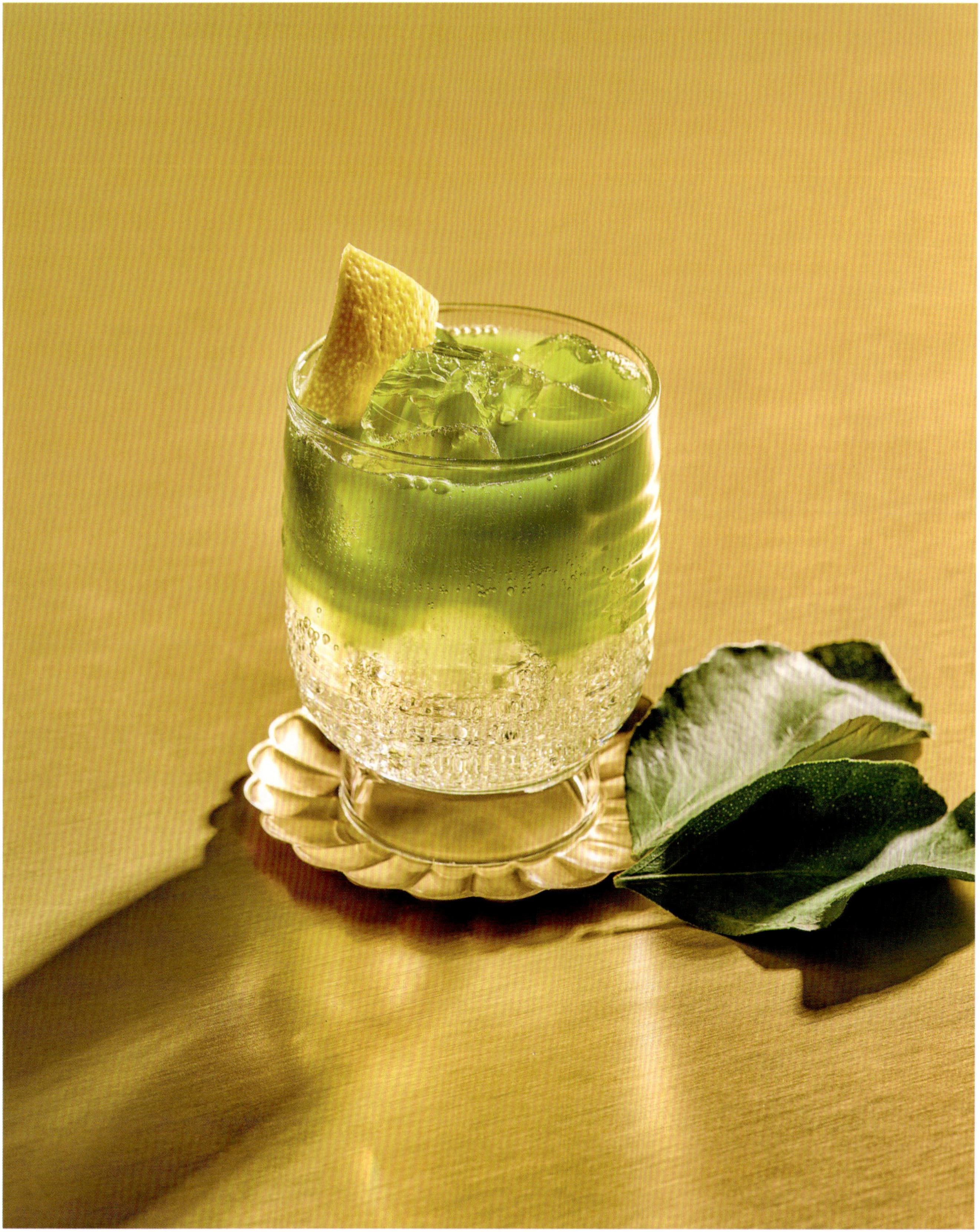

MATCHA PALMER

Brought up to date for the 21st century, this recipe uses finely ground green tea leaves for a fragrant and sophisticated twist on the classic.

1½ teaspoons matcha powder
200 ml/7 oz. filtered water, chilled
100 ml/3¾ oz. clear sparkling lemonade
off-the-shelf mint syrup, Honey Syrup (see page 124), Ginger Syrup (see page 124) or Simple Sugar Syrup (see page 123), to taste (optional)
lemon peel, to garnish

SERVES 1

Sift the matcha powder into a bowl. Add 2 tablespoons of the cold water and whisk vigorously to make a thin paste, before slowly adding the rest of the water. Whisk until all clumps disappear.

Fill a glass with ice and add the lemonade. Slowly add the matcha to create a layered effect. If you'd like it sweeter, add syrup to taste. Garnish with lemon peel.

ARNOLD PALMER

A simple combination of two summer staples, this drink was already a favourite of golfer Arnold Palmer when he ordered it at lunch at a Palm Springs golf club in the 1960s. Another patron overheard the order and requested 'that (Arnold) Palmer drink'. Its popularity grew from there.

120 ml/4 oz. lemonade (see page 58)
180 ml/6 oz. black tea, chilled
15 ml/½ oz. Simple Sugar Syrup (see page 123), or to taste
thin lemon slices, to garnish

SERVES 1

Add ice all the way to the top of a tall glass and add the lemonade. Slide thin slices of lemon onto the sides of the glass, before slowly pouring in the iced tea for a pleasant, layered effect. If you'd like it sweeter, add syrup to taste.

VARIATION:
Named after the multi-championship-winning player who helped to revolutionise women's golf, the **Patti Borg** replaces the regular lemonade with the hibiscus variety (see page 58).

PORCH DRINKS

NIMBU SODA

When looking for something that will quench both your sweet and savoury side, this Indian-style lime soda is the mocktail for you. It is a popular beverage at every chaatwalla (street vendor) from Mumbai to Kolkata.

35 ml/1 oz. freshly squeezed lime juice
2 teaspoons sugar
¼ teaspoon sea salt (kosher salt)
340 ml/12 oz. soda water, chilled
Simple Sugar Syrup (see page 123), to taste (optional)

SERVES 1

In a glass, combine the lime juice, sugar and salt together until all crystals are dissolved. Add a little of the soda water if necessary. Add ice and the rest of soda water and stir. If you would like it sweeter, add some syrup, as granulated sugar will sneak to the bottom of the glass.

NOTE:
Dissolving the sugar and salt in the lime juice before adding in the soda water keeps the drink as fizzy as possible.

SALTY CUCUMBER LIME SODA

2 tablespoons cubed cucumber (for thick-skinned, dark green cucumbers, peel and remove seeds)
¼ teaspoon sea salt (kosher salt)
35 ml/1 oz. freshly squeezed lime juice
15 ml/½ oz. Simple Sugar Syrup (see page 123)
180–220 ml/6–8 oz. soda water, as needed

SERVES 1

In a glass, add the cucumber, salt and lime juice and muddle. Add the syrup and stir. Add ice and top up with soda water.

VARIATION:
For a **Double Mint Lime Soda** substitute the Simple Sugar Syrup for off-the-shelf mint syrup and add 3–5 fresh, torn mint leaves.

PORCH DRINKS

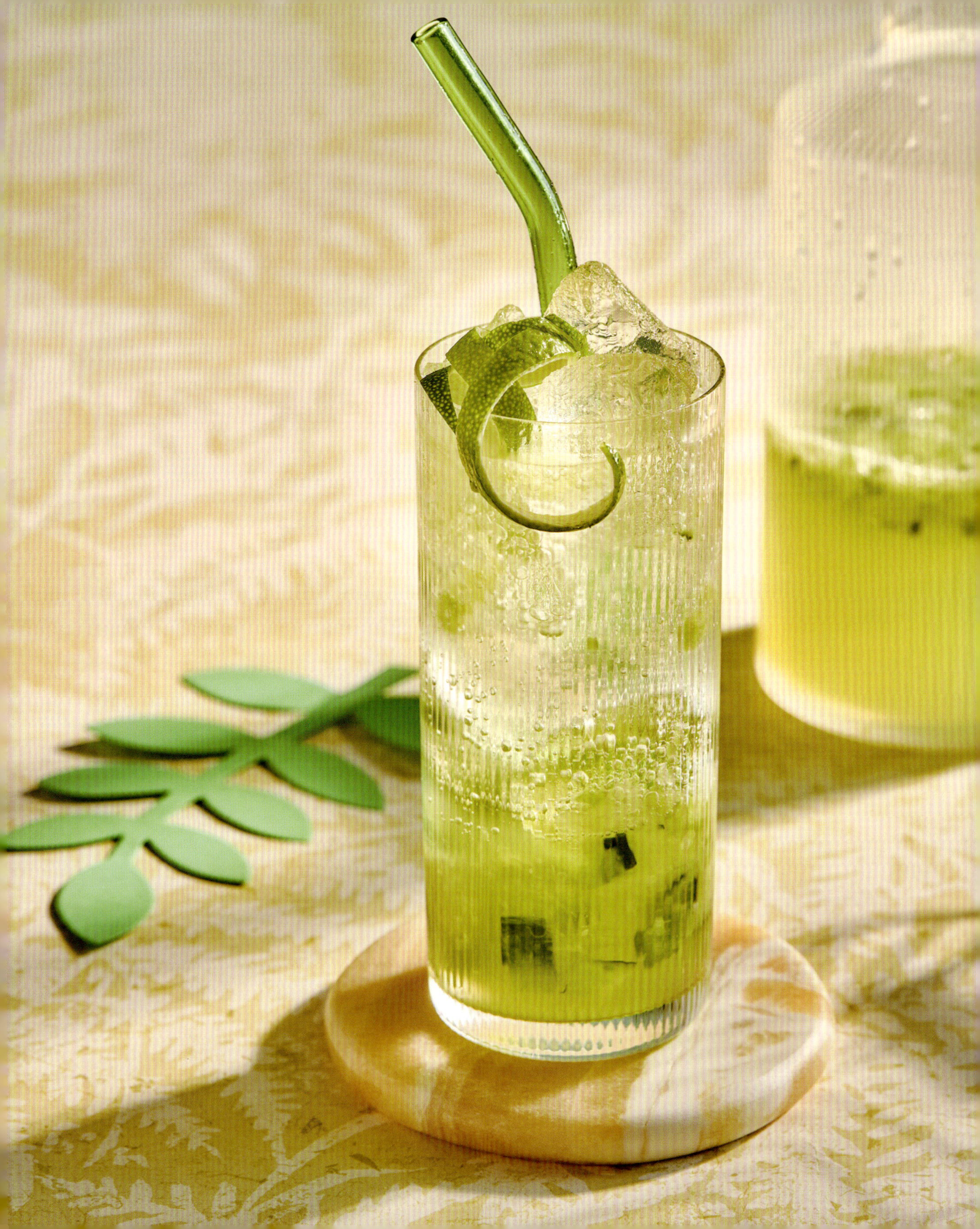

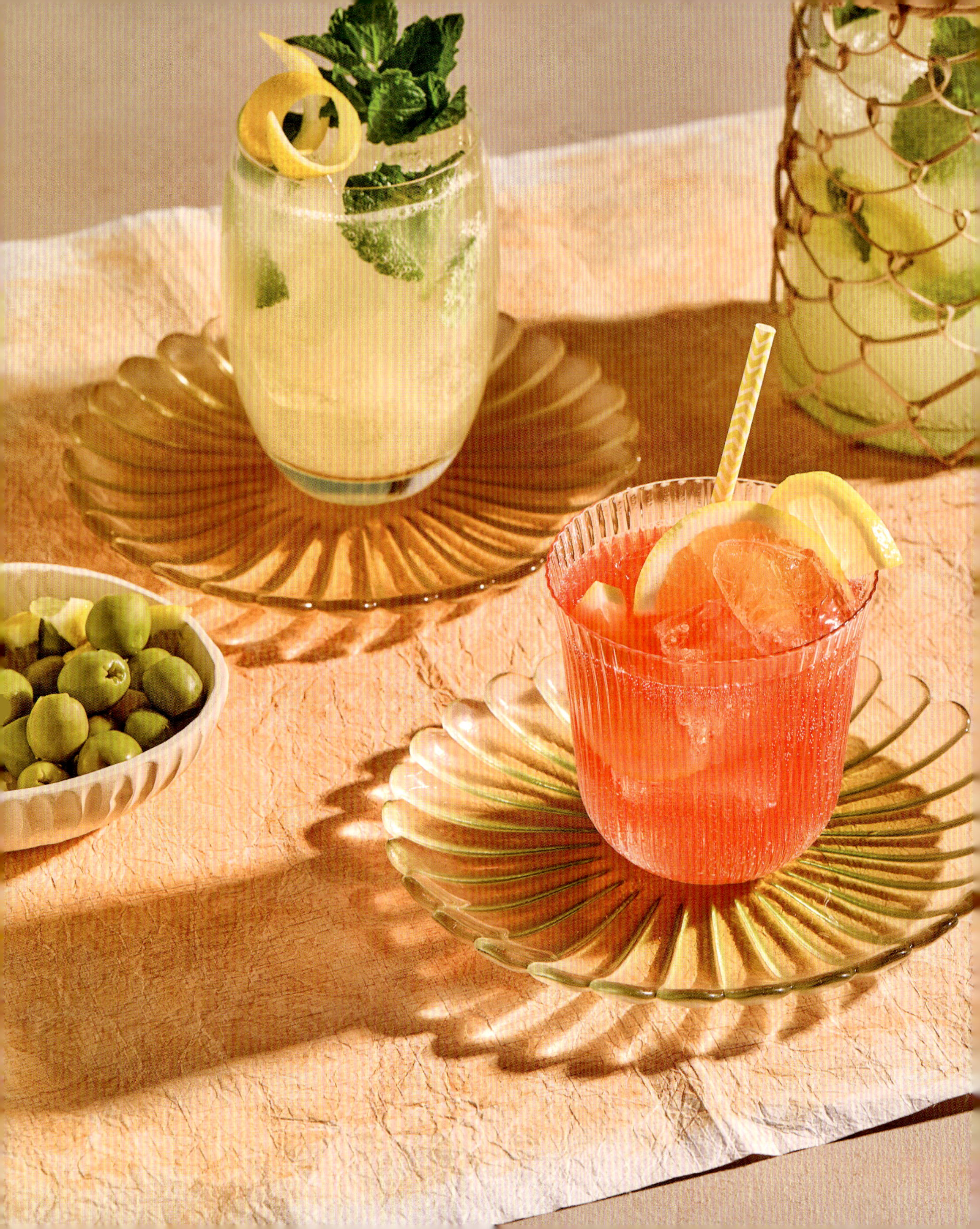

LIMONANA

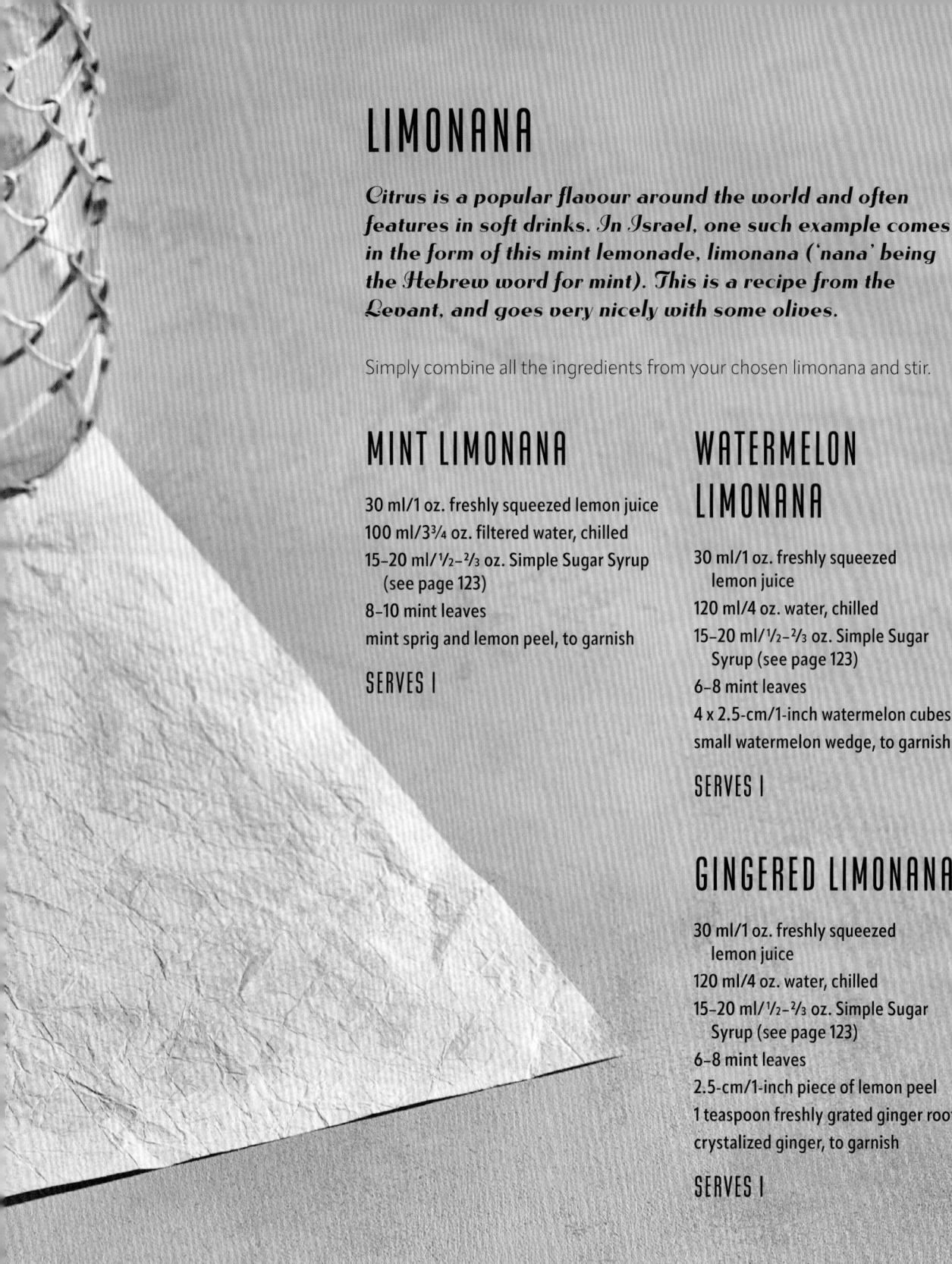

Citrus is a popular flavour around the world and often features in soft drinks. In Israel, one such example comes in the form of this mint lemonade, limonana ('nana' being the Hebrew word for mint). This is a recipe from the Levant, and goes very nicely with some olives.

Simply combine all the ingredients from your chosen limonana and stir.

MINT LIMONANA

30 ml/1 oz. freshly squeezed lemon juice
100 ml/3¾ oz. filtered water, chilled
15–20 ml/½–⅔ oz. Simple Sugar Syrup (see page 123)
8–10 mint leaves
mint sprig and lemon peel, to garnish

SERVES 1

WATERMELON LIMONANA

30 ml/1 oz. freshly squeezed lemon juice
120 ml/4 oz. water, chilled
15–20 ml/½–⅔ oz. Simple Sugar Syrup (see page 123)
6–8 mint leaves
4 x 2.5-cm/1-inch watermelon cubes
small watermelon wedge, to garnish

SERVES 1

GINGERED LIMONANA

30 ml/1 oz. freshly squeezed lemon juice
120 ml/4 oz. water, chilled
15–20 ml/½–⅔ oz. Simple Sugar Syrup (see page 123)
6–8 mint leaves
2.5-cm/1-inch piece of lemon peel
1 teaspoon freshly grated ginger root
crystalized ginger, to garnish

SERVES 1

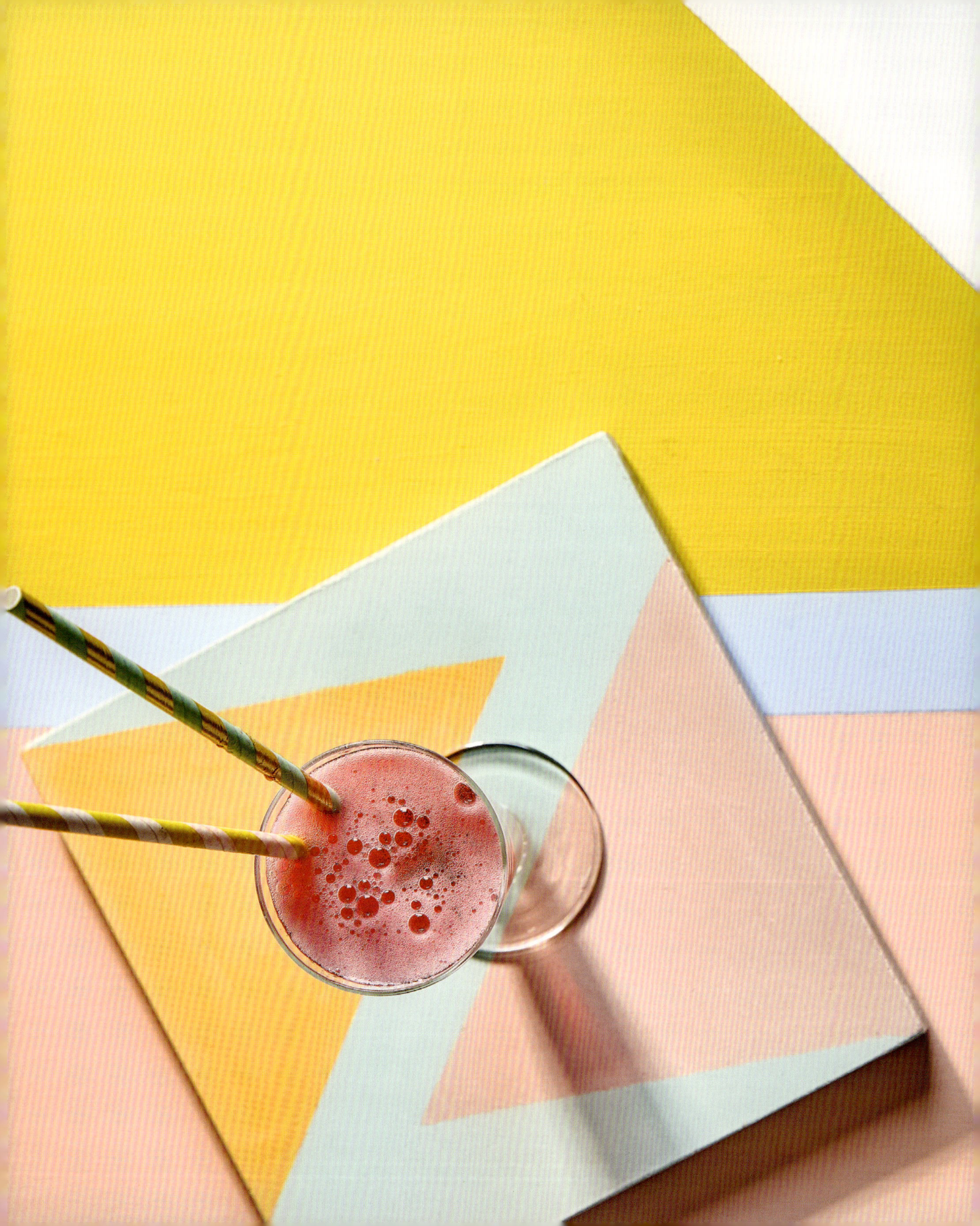

THE SODA FOUNTAIN

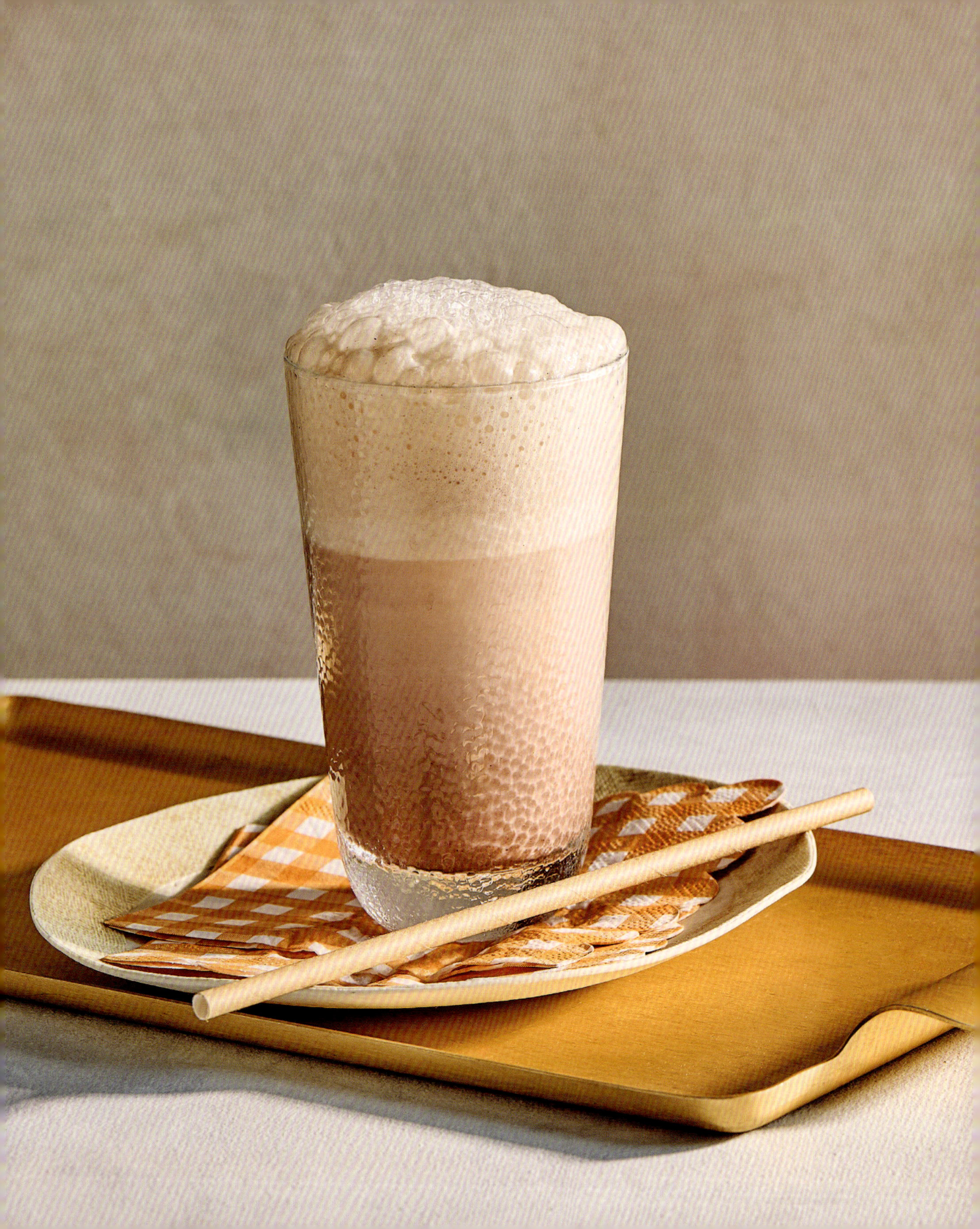

CHOCOLATE EGG CREAM

Despite the name, this drink contains neither eggs, nor cream. A staple of New York lunch counters, this drink has a refreshing effervescence and a balanced sweetness. The key to egg creams is to keep everything as cold as possible before mixing.

15 ml/½ oz. Chocolate Syrup (see page 124; not too thick)
60 ml/2 oz. milk, chilled (for non-dairy alternatives, the richer the better)
soda water, chilled (ideally unopened and highly carbonated)

SERVES 1

Take a tall, well-chilled glass, add the syrup and milk and quickly whisk until mixed. Tilt the glass slightly and pour the soda water down your stirring spoon to create a foamy head. Serve with straws.

VANILLA EGG CREAM

Use 30 ml/1 oz. Vanilla Syrup (see page 124) instead of Chocolate Syrup, and use 90 ml/3 oz. chilled milk

COFFEE EGG CREAM

Use Coffee Syrup (see page 123) instead of Chocolate Syrup or use Cold Brew Coffee Syrup (see page 123) for a lighter coffee flavour.

FRUIT EGG CREAM

Use 30 ml/1 oz. of Cherry Syrup (see page 78) or your choice of any off-the-shelf fruit syrup (strawberry, pineapple, etc.) instead of chocolate syrup.

HOMEMADE CHERRY COLA

Before the days of cola being produced in an increasing array of imaginative flavours (space-flavoured cola anyone?), there was cherry cola ~ the original variation.

15 ml/½ oz. Cherry Syrup (see below)
200 ml/7 oz. cola
cocktail cherry, to garnish

SERVES 1

Pour the Cherry Syrup into an ice-filled highball glass and add the cola. Mix to combine, garnish with a cocktail cherry and add straws.

CHERRY SYRUP
400 g/1½ cups pitted fresh cherries
300 g/1½ cups sugar
30 ml/1 oz. Simple Sugar Syrup (see page 123)

In a saucepan add the cherries, sugar and 340 ml/12 oz. water, and simmer on medium heat, stirring to dissolve sugar.

Mash the cherries as they cook (this will take 7–10 minutes) to break down the fruit. Remove from the heat and cool to room temperature. Strain out the solids and reserve the juice. Stir in the syrup, adding more to taste and for thickness, if needed. Store in the fridge for up to 1 month.

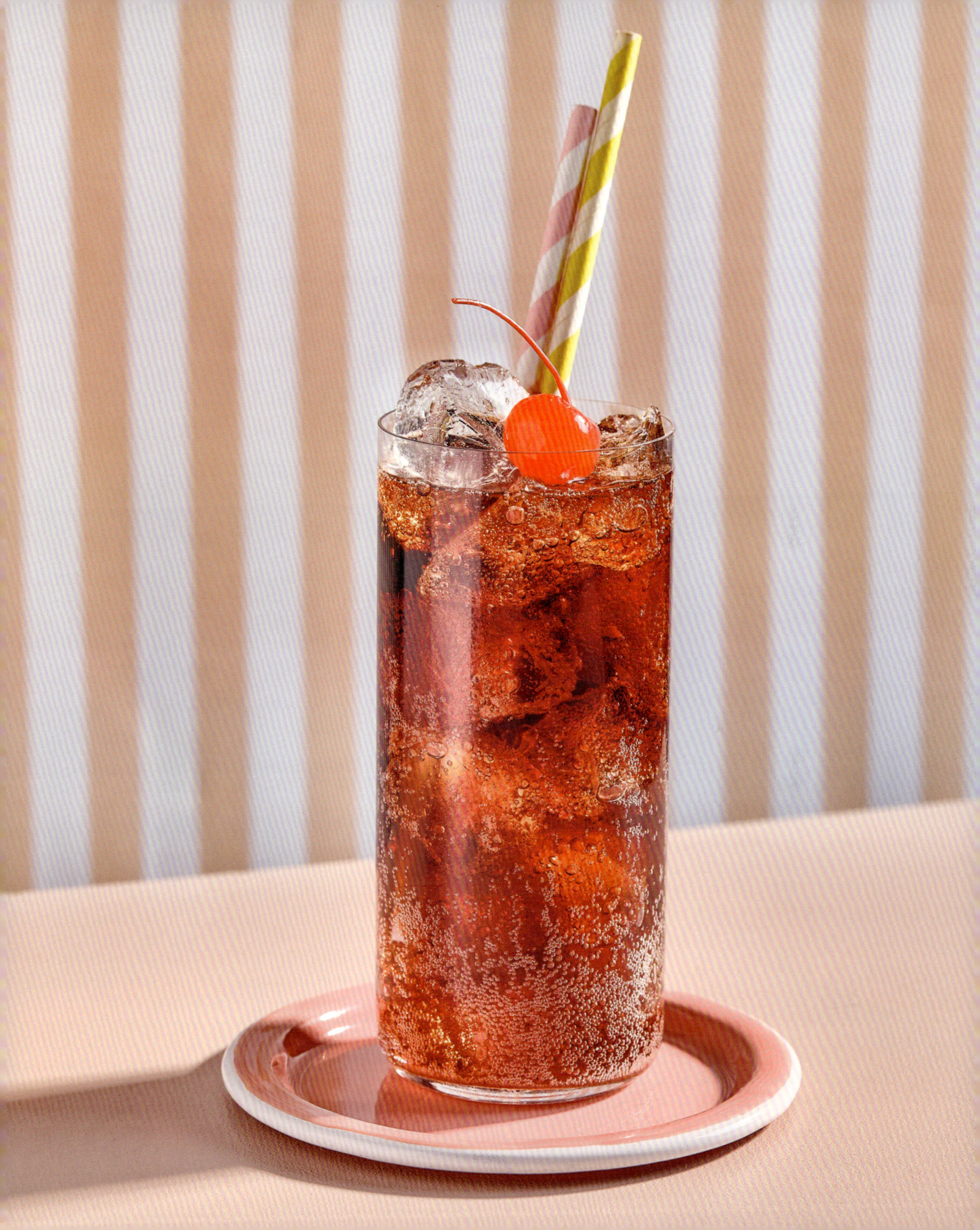

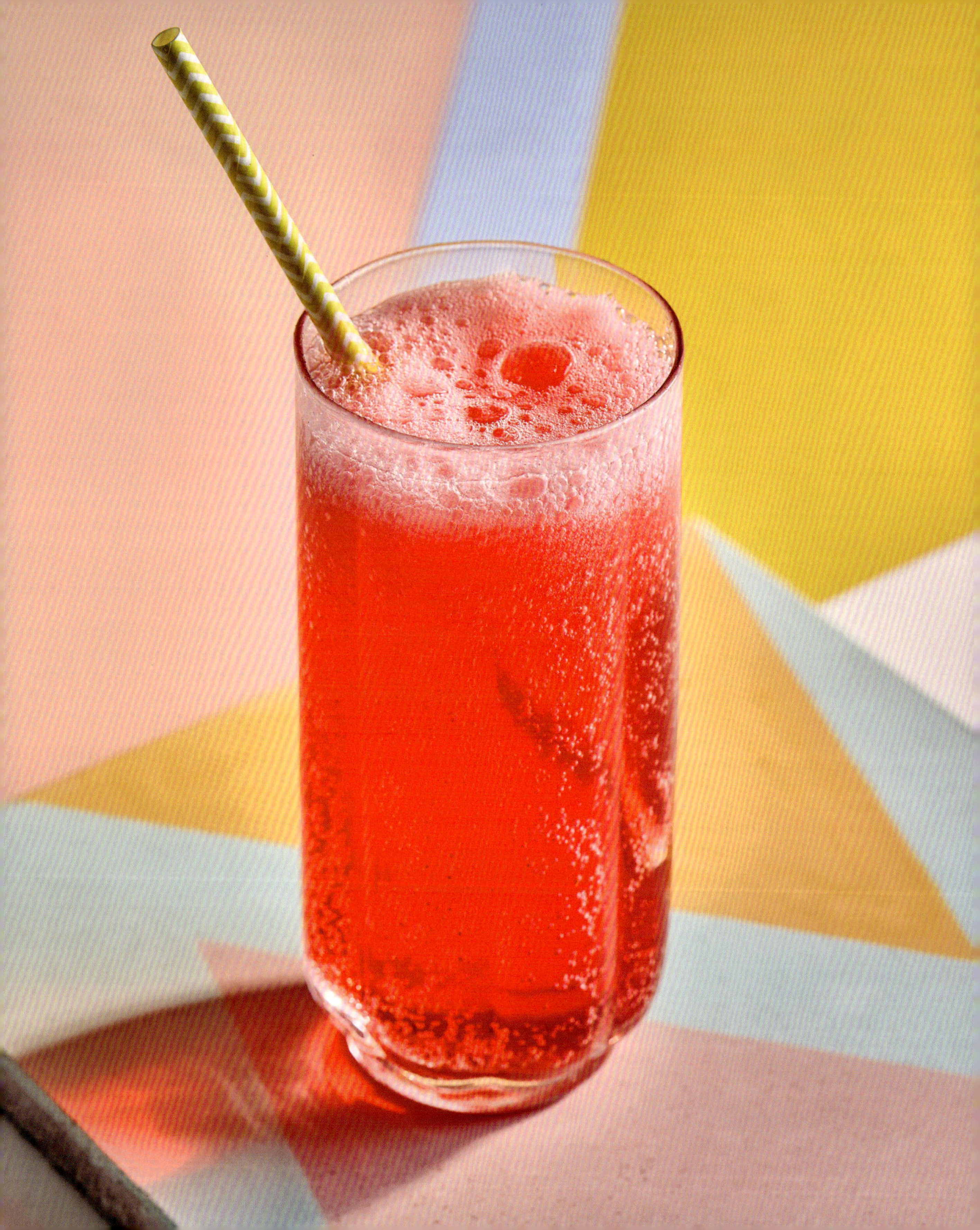

PHOSPHATE SODAS

Phosphates, a sour staple of the soda fountain for generations, may sound more like something more likely to be found in a chemistry lab than a bar, but have made a resurgence in recent years as a clever cocktail ingredient, in all their invigorating (and non-alcoholic) glory. This bright and bubbly beverage is a guaranteed crowd-pleaser.

45 ml/1½ oz. flavoured homemade or off-the-shelf fruit syrup of choice, such as Cherry Syrup (see page 78), strawberry, pineapple, mango, passionfruit, etc.)
1 teaspoon acid phosphate, or ½ teaspoon Citric Acid Solution (see page 125)
soda water, well chilled (ideally unopened and highly carbonated), to top up

SERVES 1

In a chilled highball glass, add your chosen syrup and acid and mix. Tilt the glass slightly and top up with ice-cold soda water.

The drinks have a real vibrancy from the splash of citric acid, giving them a more sophisticated, grown-up character and carrying the flavour of the syrup for a lingering finish.

NOTE:
For a refreshing afternoon boost replace the fruit syrup with Coffee Syrup (see page 123) or Chocolate Syrup (see page 124).

BOSTON COOLER

Despite its name, this drink isn't a Boston original. There is a delicious rum version dating back to late-1800s Massachusetts, which consists of rum, lime and soda water.

During the height of the American soda counter days, and the dark days of Prohibition, the term Boston Cooler became a catch-all term for a cool and refreshing beverage. Ingredients ranged from root beer, sarsaparilla, birch beer, Moxie (a cola from Maine), ice-cream, lime, melon and other fruit, rum and even ginger ale. It wasn't until 1967, when Detroit company Vernor trademarked the name 'Boston Cooler' to promote their new ice-cream bar, that the recipe including spicy ginger ale (which, in our humble opinion, is the best of the bunch) was formalized.

350 ml/12 oz. Cold Verner's Ginger Ale or other spicy ginger ale (ginger beer in a pinch)
2 scoops softened vanilla ice-cream

SERVES 1

This is a milkshake and needs to be blended. Add a little cold ginger ale to your blender along with the ice-cream. Blend at medium speed. Slowly add the rest of the ginger ale to your desired thickness. Pour into a chilled fountain glass.

NOTE:
You can also shake this cocktail with ice-cream and 60 ml/2 oz. ginger ale. If the drink starts to get too thick, start to add more ginger ale until you reach your desired thickness. If the drink gets too thin, add ice or more ice-cream.

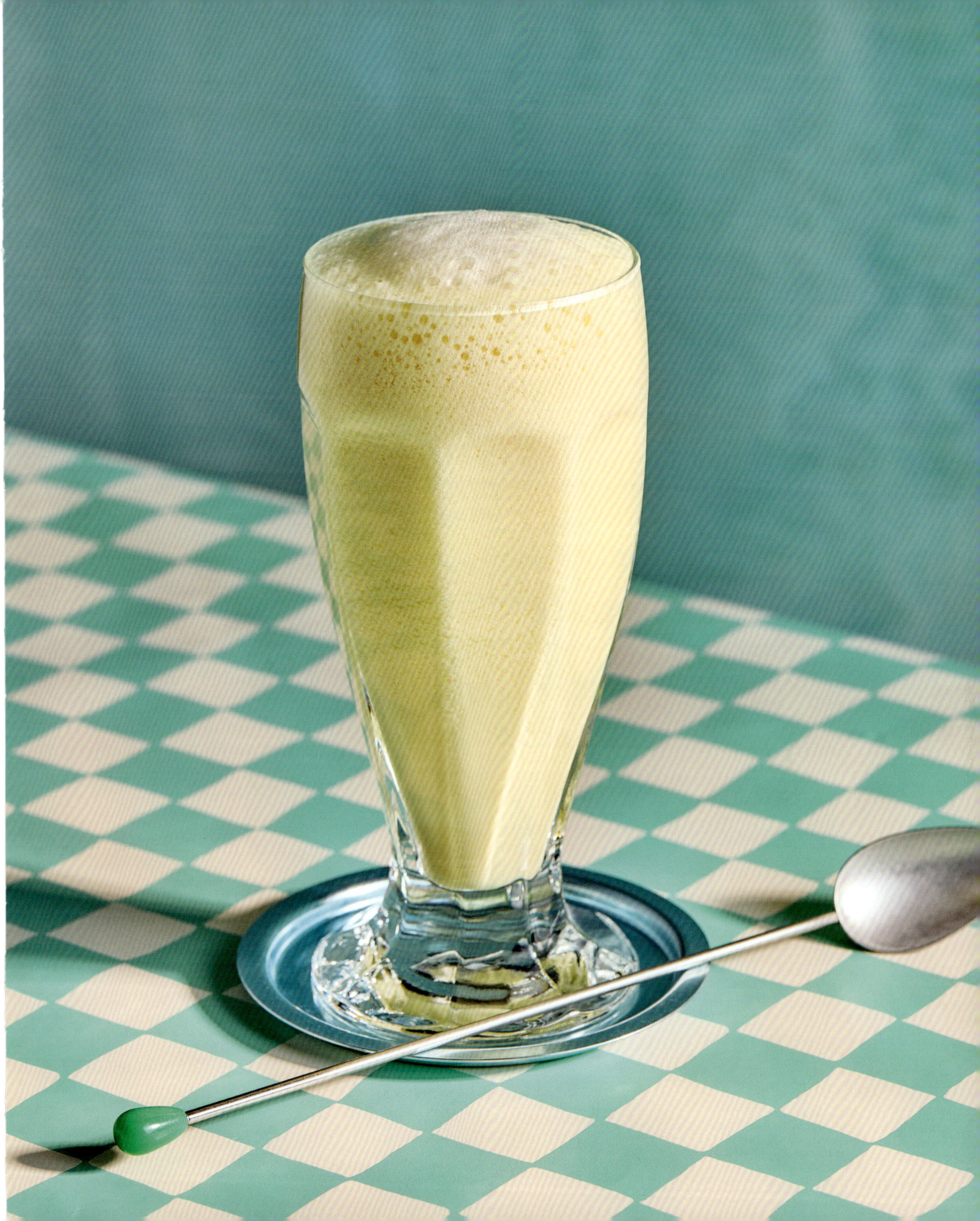

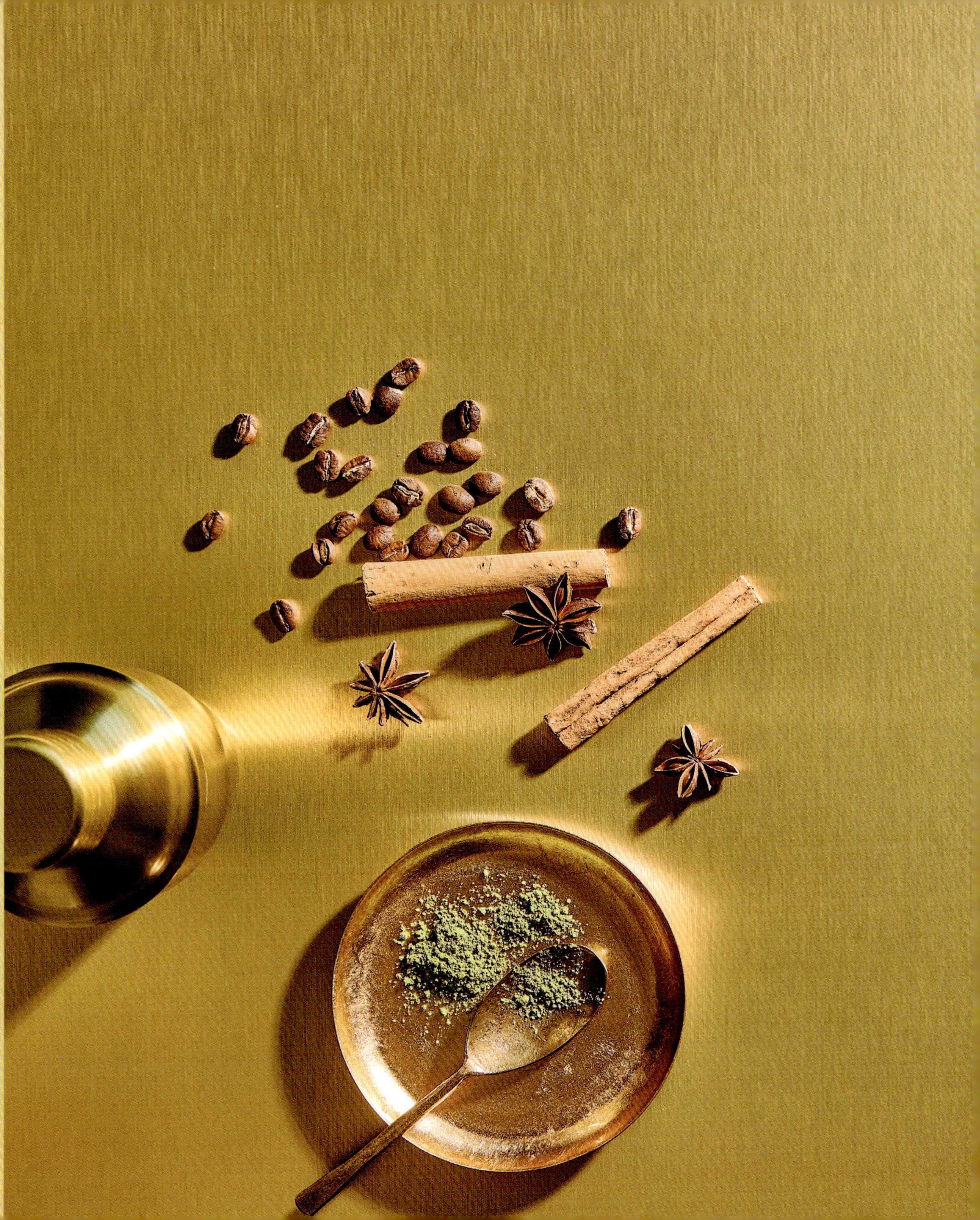

PICK-ME-UPS

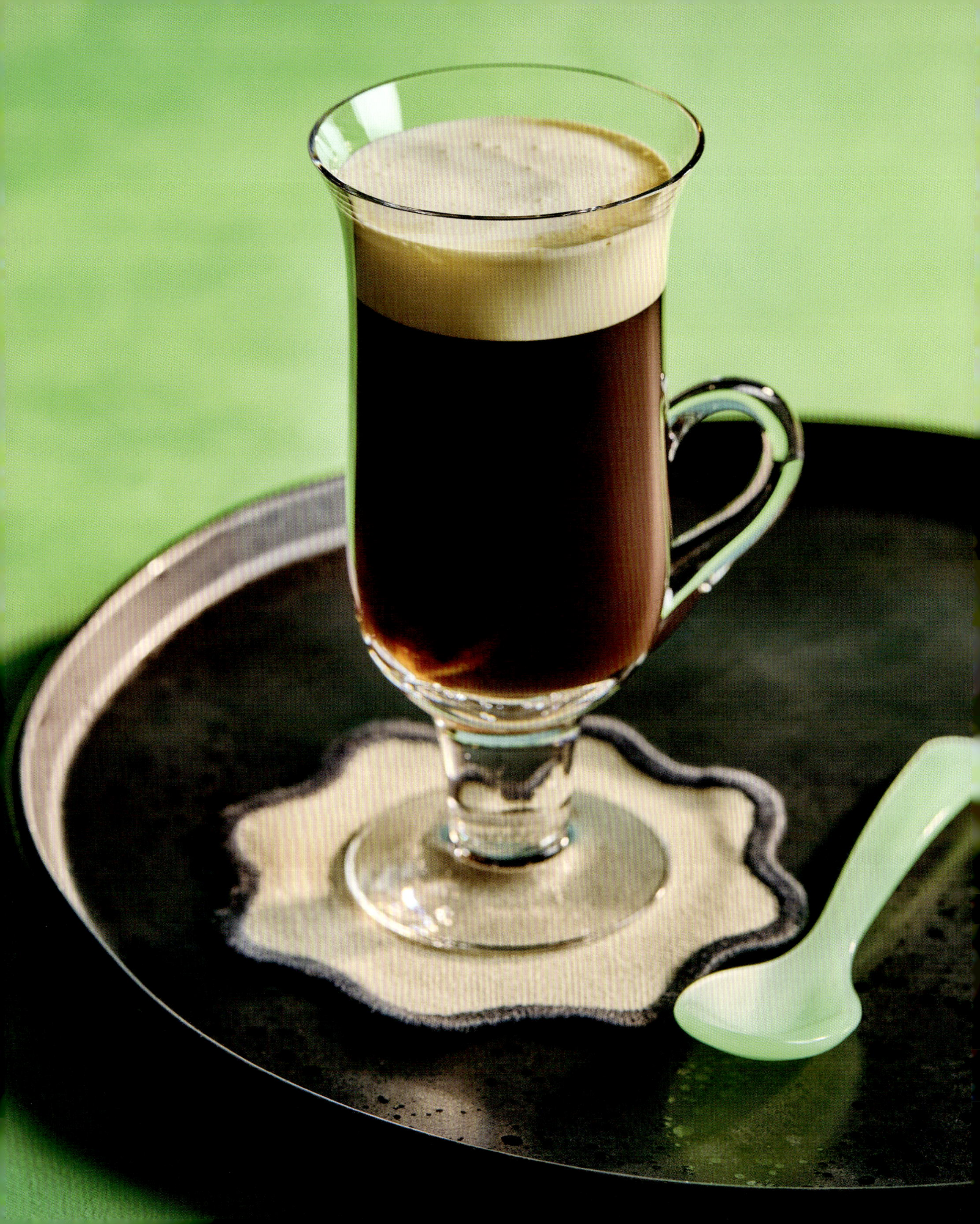

CAFE DE SHANNON

The Irish Coffee gained international popularity after being served to a group of sea-plane passengers who, bound for New York, had to return to Shannon Airport on Ireland's west coast after bad weather.

Various places around the world claim to be the home of The Irish Coffee, but one of the best is served at Bar Swift.

12 g/scant ½ oz. ground coffee
200 ml/6¾ oz. near-boiling water
3–4 tablespoons brown sugar
1–2 teaspoons Coffee Syrup (optional; see page 123)
30 ml/1 oz. double/heavy cream
50 ml/1¾ oz. Lyre's Non-alcoholic American Malt (optional)
freshly grated nutmeg or chocolate shavings, to garnish (optional)

SERVES 1

The key to the layering in an Irish Coffee is to make sure that the coffee is sweet enough. To compensate for this, the coffee needs to be stronger than normal.

Brew the coffee in the near-boiling water for 4 minutes using a cafetiere or French press. Pour into a separate jug/pitcher (ideally pre-warmed) and stir in the sugar until it dissolves. If adding coffee syrup, add it at this point.

Pour the cream into a mixing bowl and whip until thick and luxurious (this will also help with the layering).

Pre-heat coffee glasses by filling them with hot water and then pour it out. Add the whisky alternative (if using), followed by the coffee mixture. Slowly pour (or spoon) on the whipped cream so that it forms a layer on top of the coffee.

Garnish with grated nutmeg or chocolate shavings, if liked, and serve.

KAFFE & TONIC

This drink was invented in 2007 in Sweden after a staff party at Koppi Roasters in Helsingborg. It was later added to the on-site cafe's menu. Today, the drink is popular with baristas around the world.

The type of coffee used is, of course, your personal choice, but something with fruity flavours and a little acidity, perhaps from Kenya or Ethiopia, would complement the tonic water.

150–200 ml/5¼–7 oz. tonic water, as needed
50–60 ml/1¾–2 oz. espresso, cooled slightly, to taste
10–15ml/⅓–½ oz. Vanilla Syrup (see page 124) or
 Simple Sugar Syrup (see page 123), to taste
dried orange wheel, to garnish

SERVES 1

Fill a large glass with ice cubes and add the tonic, making sure to leave enough space for the coffee and syrup. Add the coffee, and finally the syrup. Some bartenders like to layer the coffee over the tonic water, but this is not essential.

Gently stir and garnish with a wheel of dried orange.

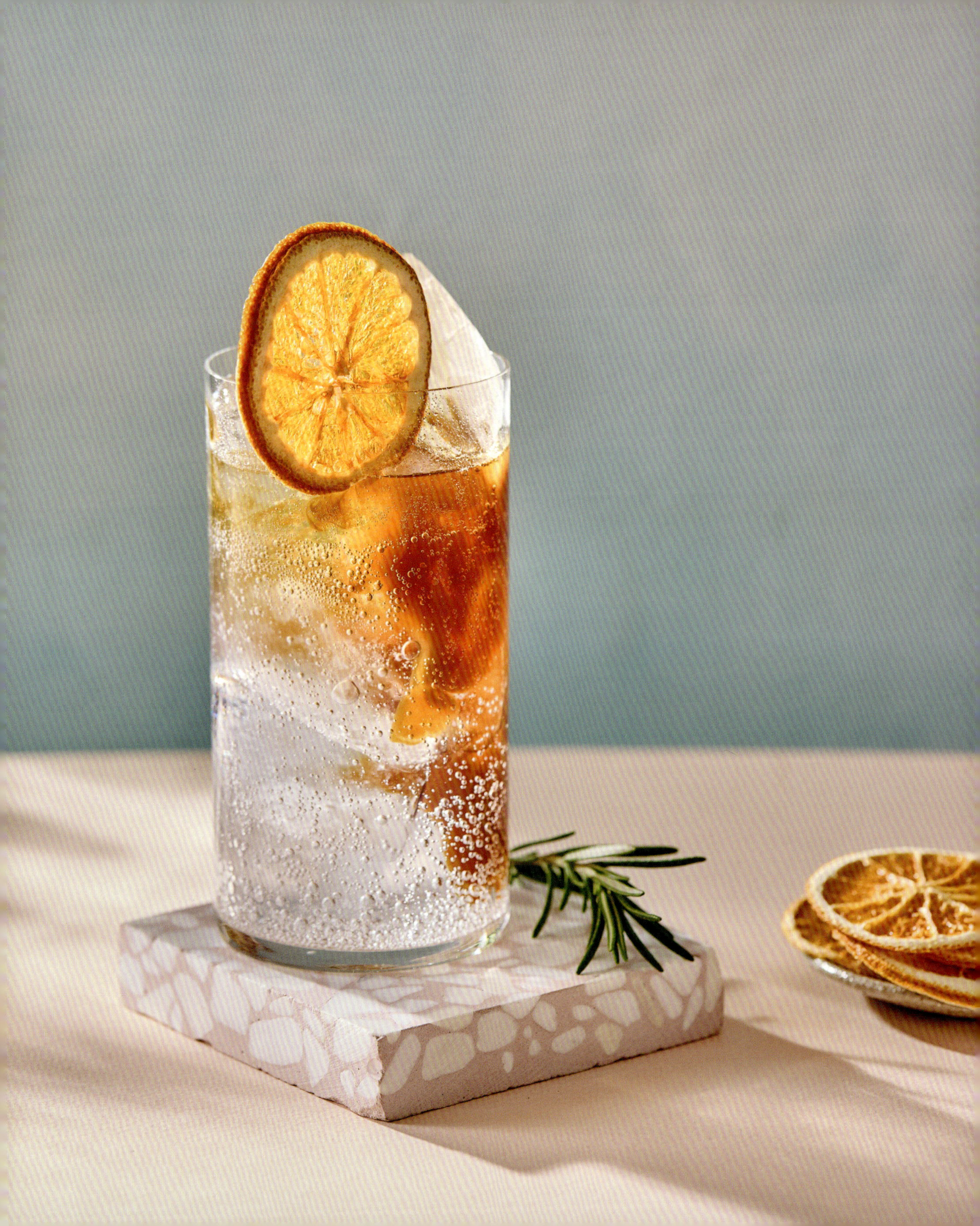

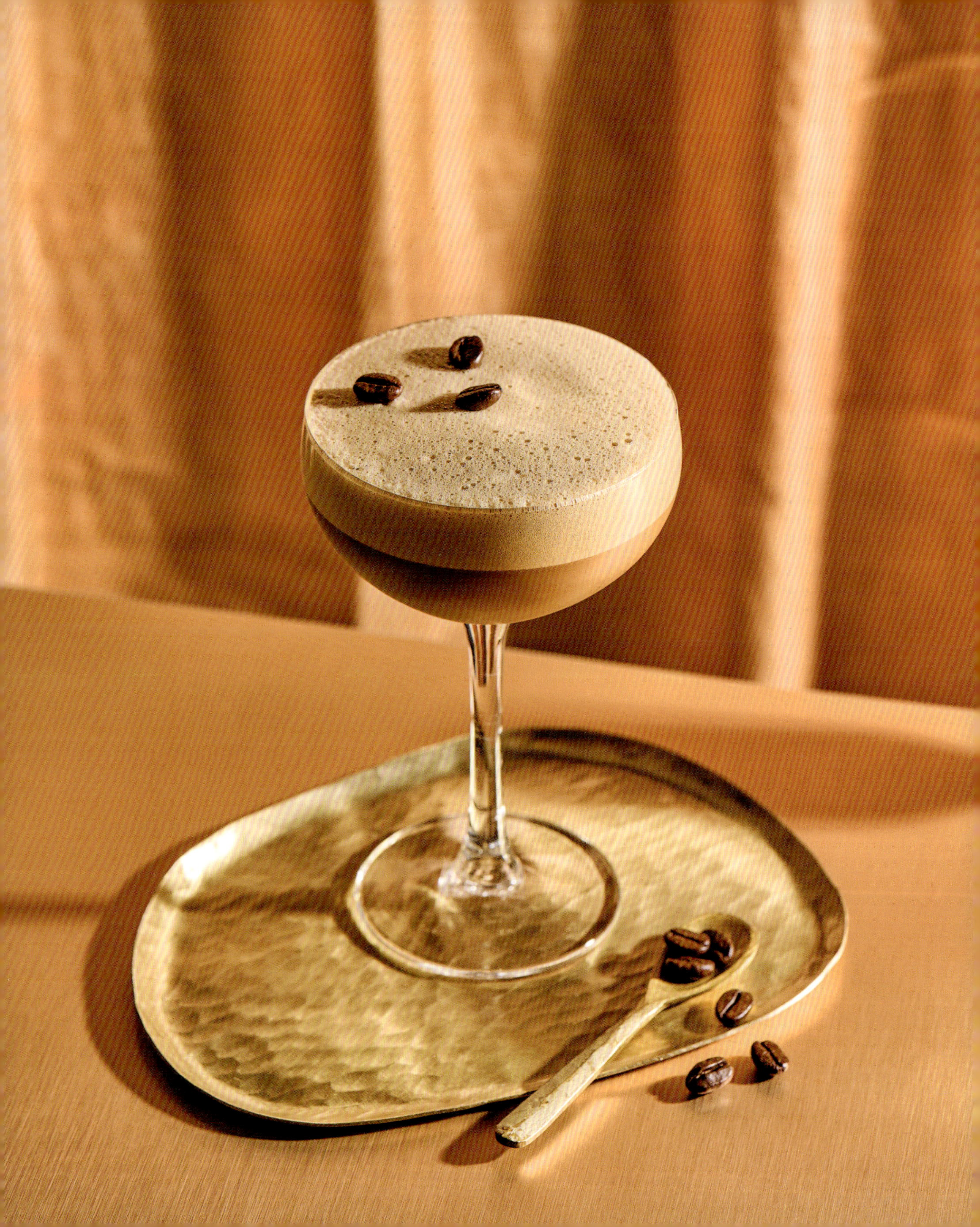

ESPRESSO LOVE

The Espresso Martini is often a popular choice to kickstart an evening out, or to provide a little livener part way through if a second wind is required. Espresso Love will do the same, but with the addition of some decadent chocolate milk, which is a great complement to the coffee.

50–60 ml/1¾–2 oz. freshly brewed espresso coffee, to taste, allowed to cool slightly
100 ml/3¾ oz. chocolate milk
10 ml/⅓ oz. Vanilla Syrup (see page 124)
3 coffee beans, to garnish

SERVES 1

Shake the ingredients vigorously in a shaker with ice and strain into a coupe or V-shaped cocktail glass . Garnish with coffee beans.

BLACK SATIN

The Black Velvet was created in 1861 at the prestigious Brooks's Club in London following the death of Prince Albert, husband to Queen Victoria. Inspired by the black armbands worn by club members, it was felt that 'even the Champagne should be in mourning'. This version combines 0% Guinness and non-sparkling alcoholic wine to great effect.

75 ml/2½ oz. 0% Guinness (Irish dark stout)
75 ml/2½ oz. non-alcoholic sparkling wine

SERVES 1

Add the ingredients to a champagne flute or, if available, a small pewter tankard if available. No garnish is needed.

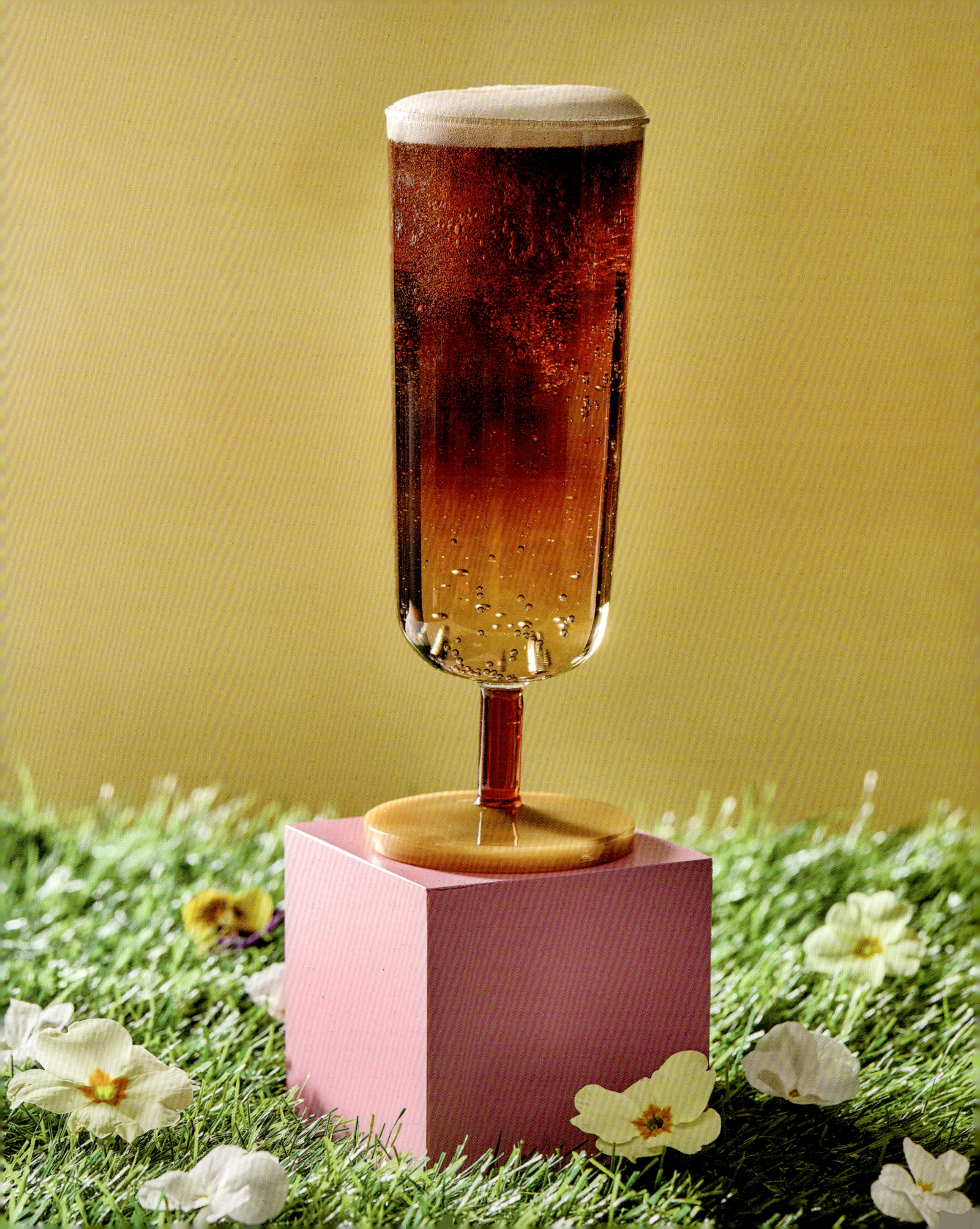

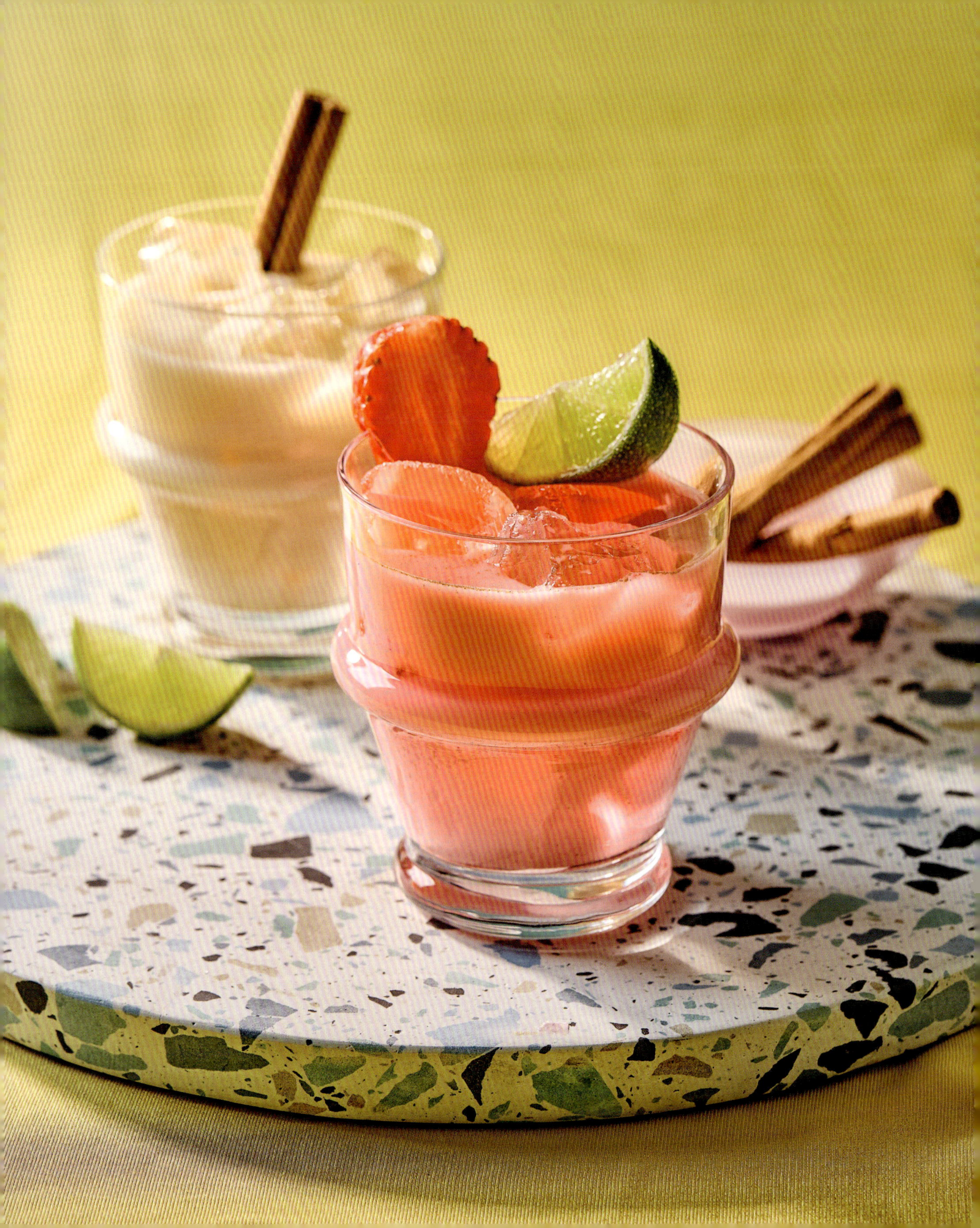

HORCHATA

Horchata is usually made by soaking uncooked white rice overnight, blending and straining it through muslin/cheesecloth, keeping only the liquid. It is truly a labour of love. Below is a cheat that results in a pretty good facsimile.

6 tablespoons sugar
2 teaspoons vanilla powder or use 1½ tablespoons vanilla extract and 30 ml/1 oz. Vanilla Syrup (see page 124)
½ teaspoon ground sweet cinnamon
240 ml/8½ oz. full-fat/whole milk (or use oat milk or almond milk for a nuttier version)
1.5 litres/quarts Unsweetened Rice Milk (see below)
cinnamon sticks, to garnish

SERVES 6

In a large vessel add the sugar, vanilla powder (or substitute) and the cinnamon. Add the milk and stir, before tasting for sweetness. Adjust to taste. Store in the fridge for 1 week.

To serve, fill a tumbler with ice and pour in the mixture. Garnish each serving with a cinnamon stick.

UNSWEETENED RICE MILK
1.5 litres/quarts warm water
600 g/3 cups risotto rice

Mix the warm water and risotto rice and blend for 90 seconds. Strain and use immediately, or, for best results, allow the mixture's flavours to marry overnight before straining out the rice pulp. Keep refrigerated.

DIRTY HORCHATA

Add 30 ml/1 oz. espresso to an ice-filled glass before adding 200 ml/7 oz. horchata.

SERVES 1

PINK HORCHATA

Add 25–50 ml/1–2 oz. off-the-shelf strawberry syrup to an ice-filled glass, add 200 ml/7 oz. horchata and stir. Garnish with a fresh strawberry slice and lime wedge (optional).

SERVES 1

ICED HONG KONG MILK TEA

Hong Kong Milk Tea is usually made by 'pulling' the hot tea in a silk sock four times to remove the astringency of the tea's robust flavours. A similar result can be achieved using a batch of cold brew tea.

30 ml/1 oz. sweetened condensed milk
15 ml/½ oz. Rich Simple Sugar Syrup (see page 123)
250 ml/9 oz. Cold Brew Black Tea (see below)

SERVES 1

Coat the inside of a large glass with half of the condensed milk, before adding ice and the syrup. Pour in the remaining condensed milk. Add the tea and stir to combine.

COLD BREW BLACK TEA
1 tablespoon Assam loose-leaf tea
1 tablespoon Ceylon loose-leaf tea
950 ml/32 oz. filtered water, chilled

Add the tea leaves and filtered water to a clean, airtight glass container and place in the refrigerator for 8–12 hours. Strain out the leaves and keep covered at room temperature for up to 3 days. Do not refrigerate, as this causes it to go cloudy.

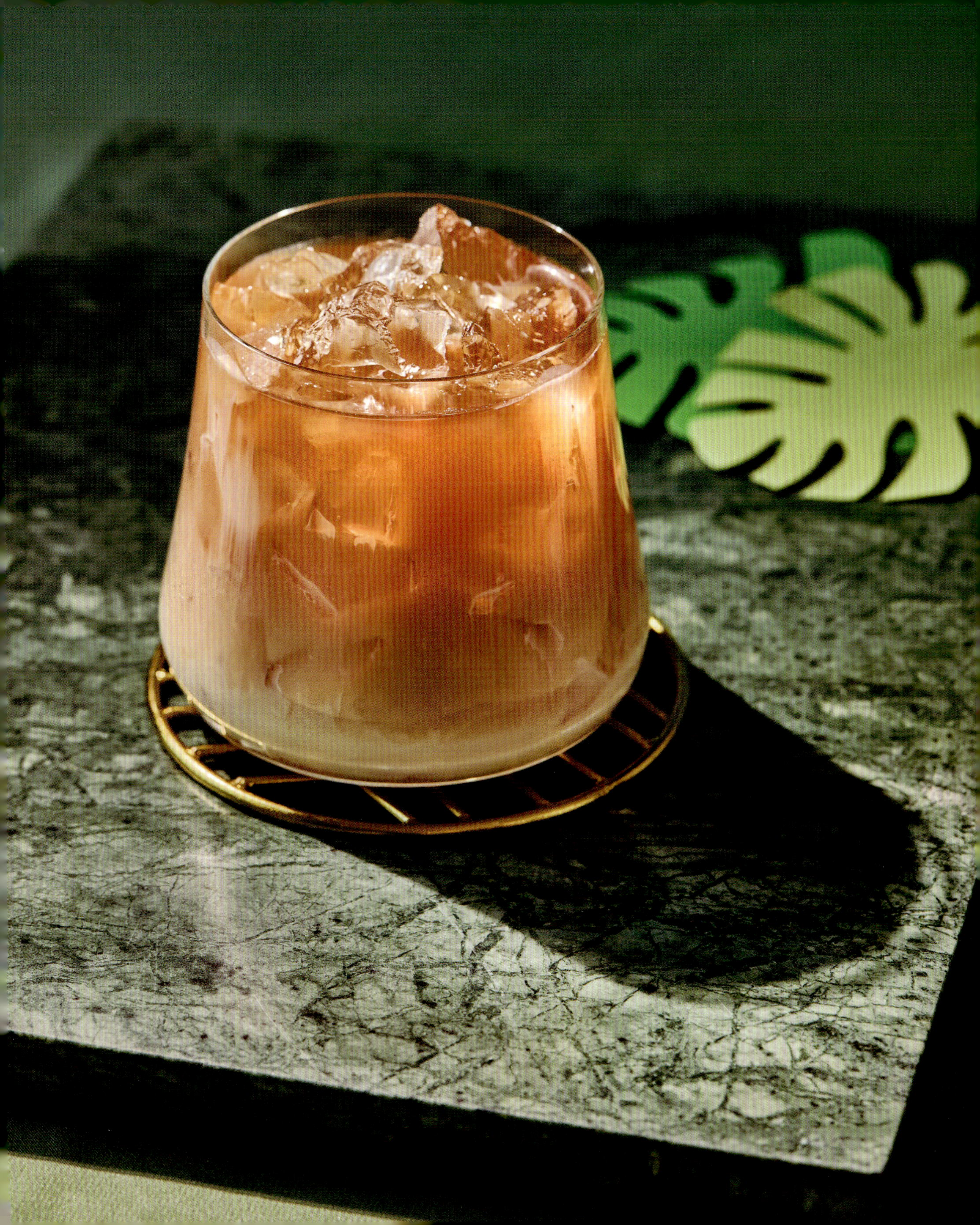

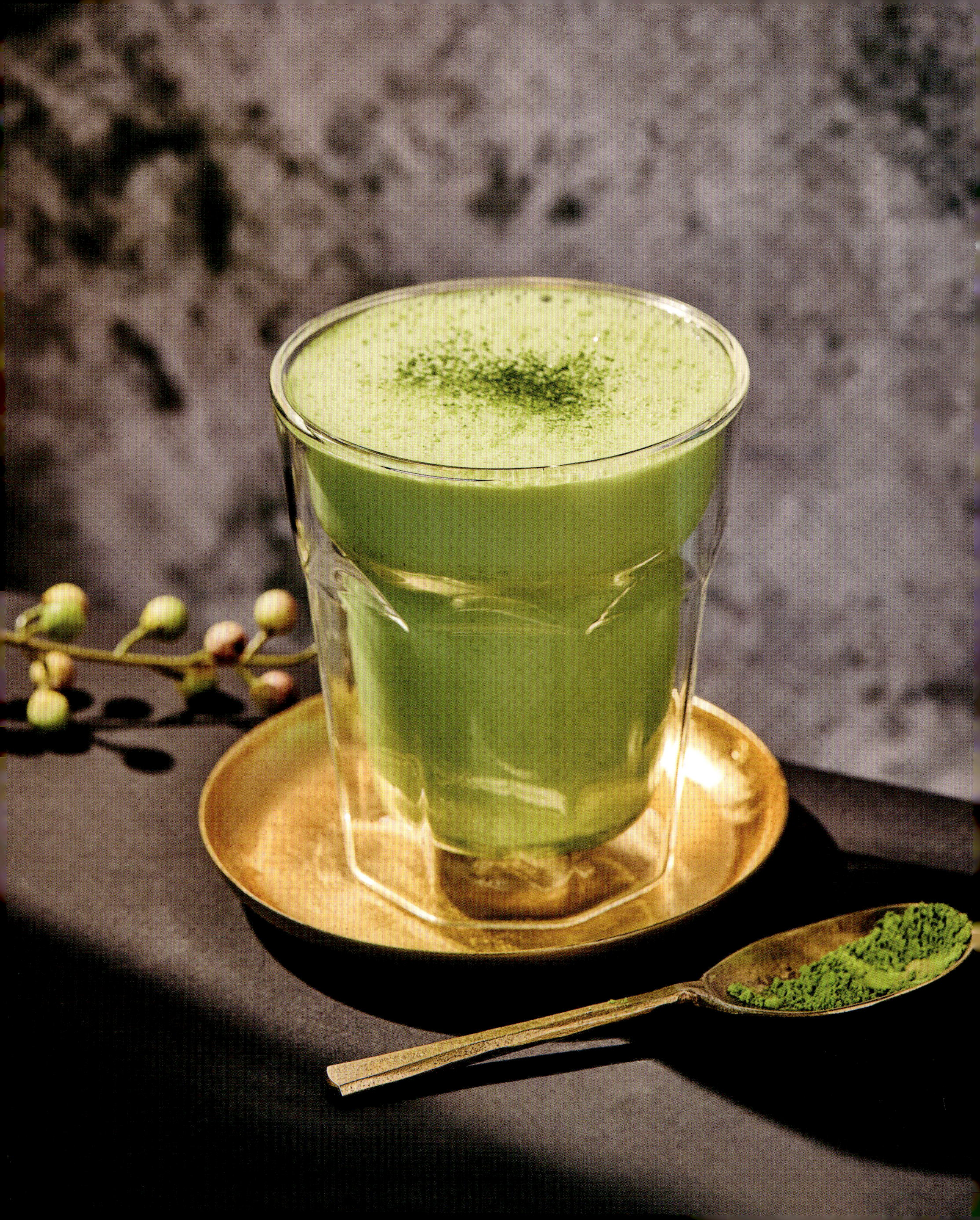

MATCHA LATTE

Matcha, a powder made from ground green tea leaves, has two main grades: ceremonial and culinary. Ceremonial grade is produced from the season's first harvest. The leaves are young and have more chlorophyll, hence they have the most vibrant colour. The stems and veins are removed prior to the grinding process, making for a sweeter flavour and finer texture.

Culinary grade is harvested later in the season. These leaves have been subjected to more sunlight. They are ground into a slightly coarse powder that is earthy and bitter. Culinary grade has a bolder flavour and can stand up well to combining with other ingredients.

Traditionally, a bamboo whisk is used to make matcha tea, but a regular metal whisk will work just fine. To get a frothy finish, whip the milk with a milk frother.

1½ teaspoons matcha powder
1 tablespoon hot water
30 ml/1 oz. Honey Syrup (see page 124)
25 ml/¾ cup hot milk (or use a dairy-free alternative)

SERVES 1

Sift the matcha powder into a mug or coffee cup. Add the hot water and whisk until there are no lumps, then add the honey syrup. Add the milk and whisk together until frothy. Serve at once.

ICED STRAWBERRY MATCHA LATTE

1½ teaspoons matcha powder
60 ml/2 oz. hot water, or as needed
4–6 strawberries, sliced
60 ml/2 oz. off-the-shelf strawberry syrup
480 ml/6 oz. milk (or use a dairy-free alternative)

SERVES 1

Sift the matcha powder into a bowl. Add 30 ml/1 oz. of the hot water and whisk to make a smooth paste. Add the rest of the hot water and mix until there are no clumps and it is the consistency of yogurt; add more hot water if needed. Set aside to cool.

Add the strawberries and syrup to a glass, then fill with ice. Slowly add the milk, then gently pour the matcha over the milk to keep the layers separate.

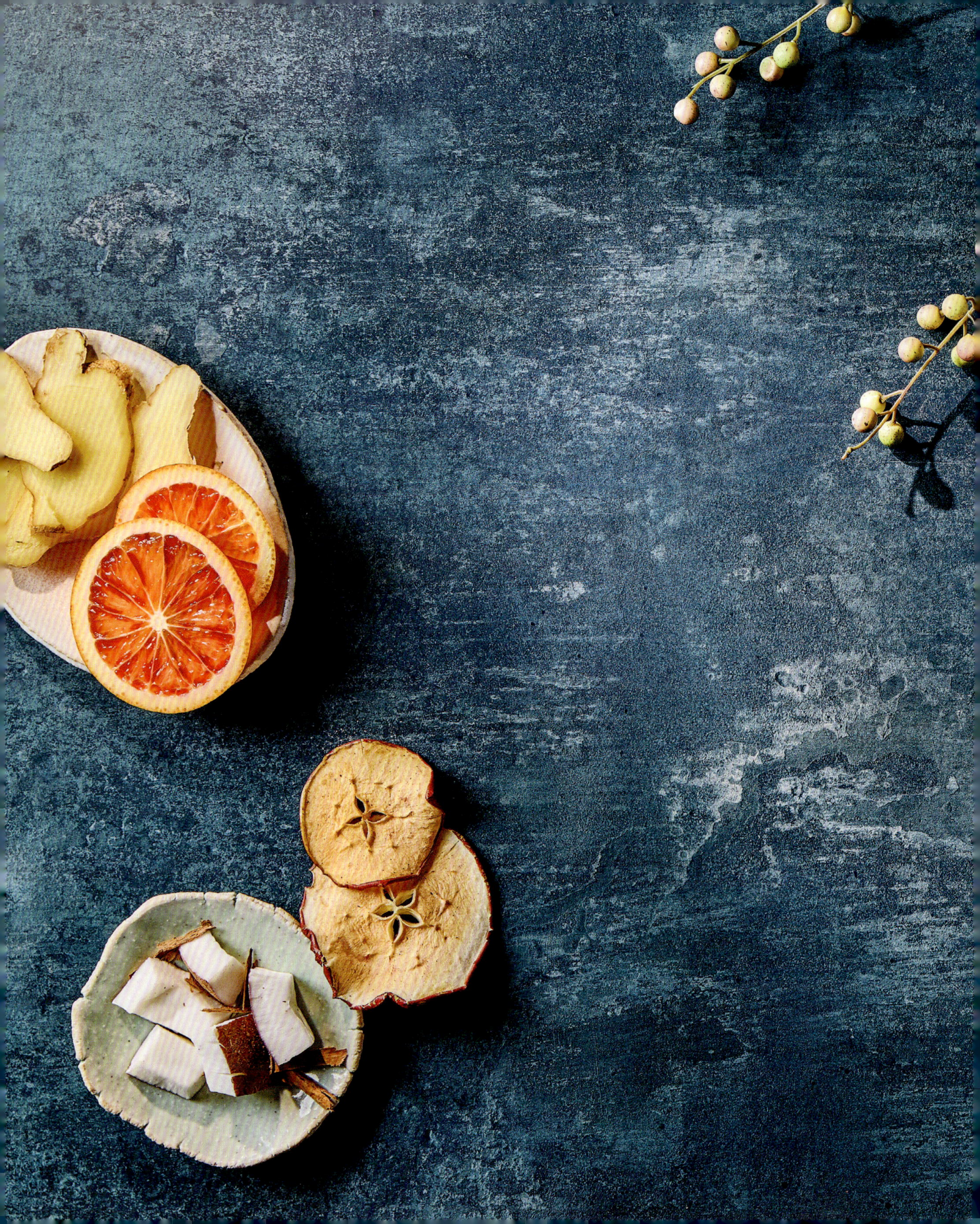

SEASONAL SPECIALS

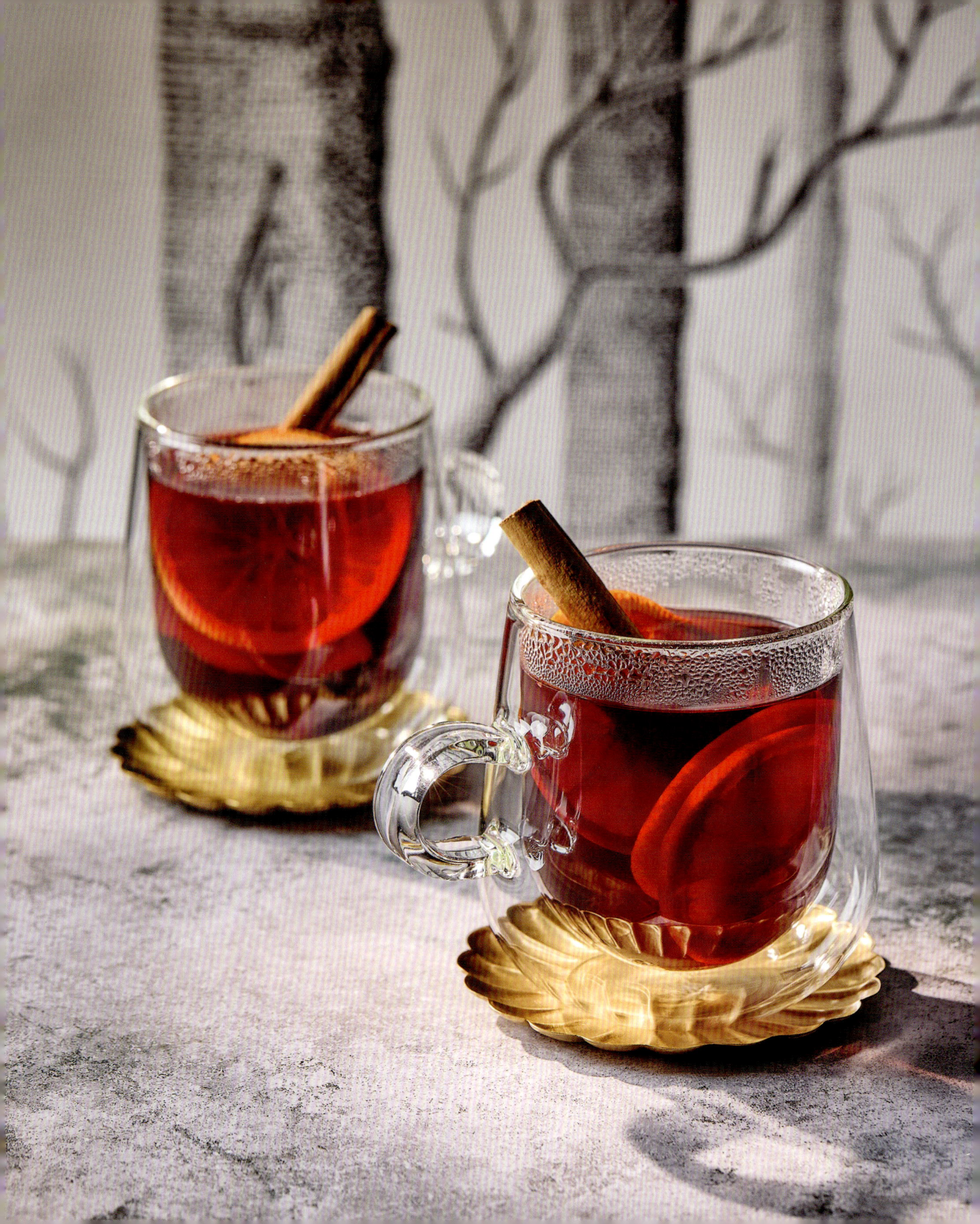

MULLED DRINKS

Hot spiced drinks have a history stretching back nearly 1,000 years with wassailing. This noisy English practice takes place in an orchard – people sing, shout and bang pots and pans to scare away bad spirits and bless the fruitful harvest.

MULLED WINE

500 ml/17 oz. non-alcoholic red wine
15 ml/½ oz. red wine vinegar
1 orange, sliced
5–10 cloves
1 cinnamon stick
10 g/⅓ oz. ginger root, sliced
50 ml/1½ oz. Vanilla Syrup (see page 124)
cinnamon sticks, to garnish

SERVES 2

In a saucepan, combine all the ingredients and bring to a gentle simmer. Ladle into heatproof glasses and garnish each serving with a cinnamon stick.

MULLED CIDER

500 ml/17 oz. cloudy apple juice
15 ml/½ oz. apple cider vinegar
1 apple, cored and sliced
3 tablespoons brown sugar
2 teaspoons sweet ground cinnamon
20 ml/¾ oz. Vanilla Syrup (see page 124)
dried apple slices, to garnish

SERVES 2

In a saucepan, combine the ingredients and bring to a gentle simmer. Ladle into heatproof glasses and garnish each serving with a dried apple slice.

SEASONAL SPECIALS

HOT BUTTERED APPLE

This drink is the liquid crossover of a toffee apple and homemade apple pie, with an indulgent, silky texture courtesy of the butter.

200 ml/7 oz. cloudy apple juice
2 teaspoons brown sugar
1 teaspoon butter or non-dairy alternative
mixed spice/baking spices, to taste
dried apple slices, to garnish

In a saucepan, heat the apple juice until hot. Stir in the brown sugar and butter (or non-dairy alternative), as well as a sprinkle of baking spices such as cinnamon, ginger and clove.

Serve from a heatproof jug/pitcher and garnish each serving with a dried apple slice.

SERVES 1

HOT TODDY

A 'toddy', the quintessential winter warmer, whether out at a festive market or snuggling up after a bracing walk. A lovely balance of sweet and citrus with a pleasant zing of ginger.

60 ml/2 oz. Honey Syrup (see page 124)
30 ml/1 oz. Ginger Syrup (see page 124)
30 ml/1 oz. freshly squeezed lemon juice
hot water, to top up
cinnamon stick, to garnish

Add the ingredients to a heatproof mug or coffee cup and top up with hot water. Stir and garnish with a cinnamon stick.

SERVES 1

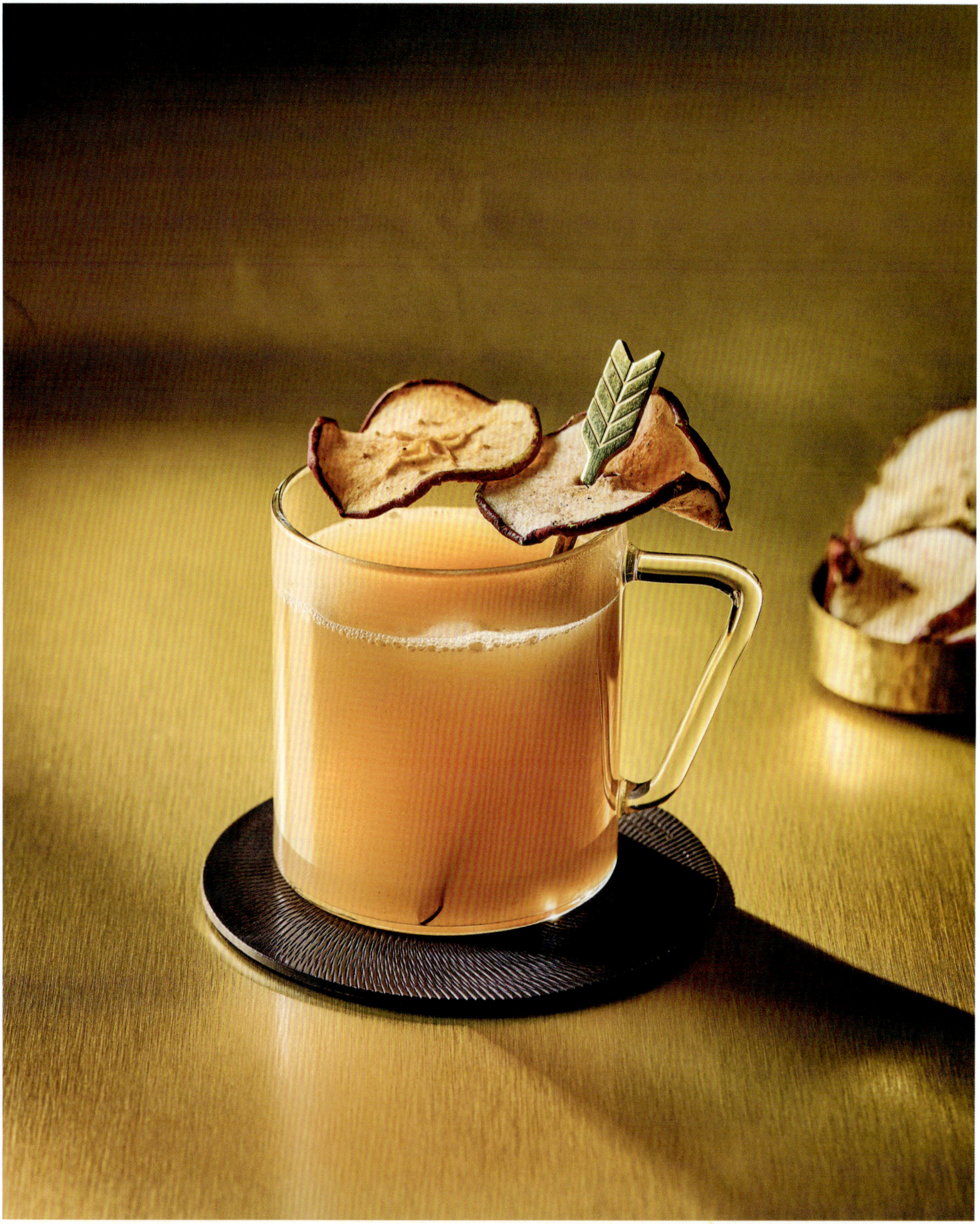

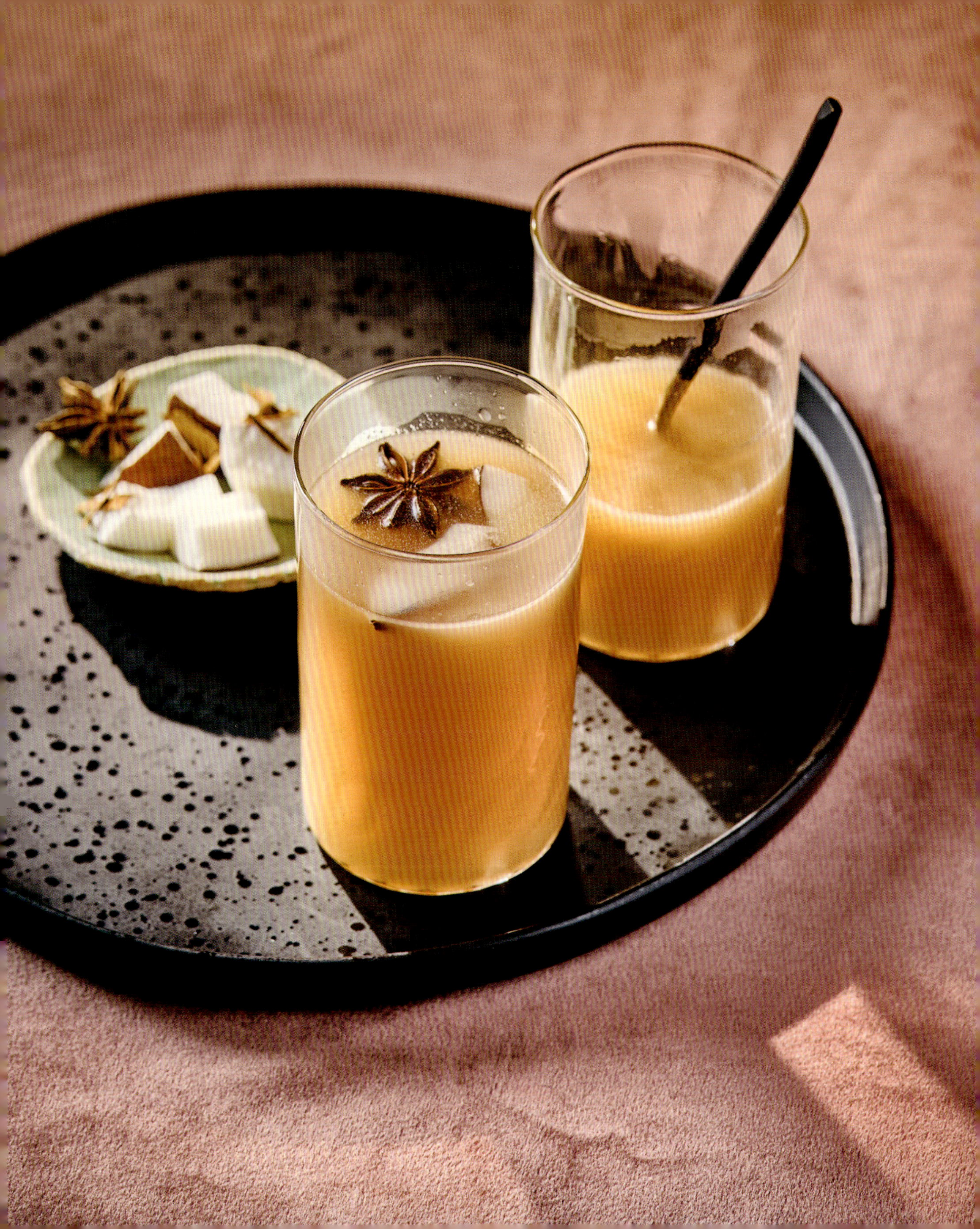

CHAI TEA LATTE

Chai is a combination of spices dating back thousands of years and originates from India. The spices often include: cinnamon, cardamom, cloves, ginger, vanilla and anise, amongst others. Each blend is unique. Chai Lattes came to the US around the 1960s, but were popularized in the 1990s by Starbucks and, in the UK, in the early 2000s.

- 950 ml/1 quart water
- 10-cm/4-inch piece ginger root, peeled, or ¼ teaspoon ground ginger
- 2–3 chai tea bags (masala chai works well)
- 240 ml/8½ oz. single/light cream (or use a dairy-free alternative)
- 4 tablespoons Rich Simple Sugar Syrup (see page 123), or to taste

SERVES 4

In a small saucepan on low–medium heat combine the water and ginger. If using fresh ginger, cover and heat for 15 minutes, but if using ground ginger, heat only for 5 minutes. Remove from the heat, add your tea bags, and steep for 5 minutes. At this point, you can strain and keep refrigerated for 7 days.

To serve, heat and divide evenly into heatproof glasses. Mix the cream and syrup and heat on low until warm, then divide between each serving.

VARIATION:
For a **Vanilla Chai Latte**, follow the recipe as above but use 3 tablespoons of Vanilla Syrup (see page 124) instead of the Rich Simple Sugar Syrup; it is sweeter so you may need to use less of it.

COCONUT CHAI TEA

- 350 ml/12 oz. Chai Tea Latte, minus the cream (see above)
- 1 tablespoon coconut oil
- 1 tablespoon unsweetened coconut cream
- Simple Sugar Syrup (see page 123), Honey Syrup (see page 124) or honey to sweeten (optional)
- star anise and pieces of fresh coconut, to garnish

SERVES 1

Heat the chai tea and add to a heatproof glass. Add the coconut oil and unsweetened coconut cream, plus sweetener to taste. Stir thoroughly until the oil is incorporated. Serve hot or cold. If serving cold, allow to cool before pouring over ice. Garnish with star anise and coconut.

SEASONAL SPECIALS

HOT BUTTERSCOTCH

Decadence and indulgence in a glass. This drink has a luxurious, velvety texture with a buttery richness balanced out by just a hint of saltiness. Incredibly moreish, it's a hug in a glass or, as the Danish may describe it, 'hygge' aka cosiness.

6 Werther's Original butter (hard) candies
100 ml/3¾ oz. filtered water
aerosol whipped cream, to serve

SERVES 1

Place the butter candies in a small microwaveable jug/pitcher with the water. Heat on full power for 60 seconds in a microwave (800W; adjust accordingly). Stir, then heat for another 60 seconds. (If you don't have a microwave add 120 ml/2 oz. boiling water and stir until melted.) Pour into a warmed drinking vessel and garnish with a dollop of whipped cream.

SWEATER WEATHER HOT BUTTERSCOTCH

90 ml/3 oz. hot butterscotch (see above)
30 ml/1 oz. off-the-shelf gingerbread syrup
120 ml/4 oz. milk (or use a dairy-free alternative)

SERVES 1

Warm the ingredients in a saucepan on the stove and stir, being careful not to overheat. Pour into a warmed heatproof drinking vessel and garnish with a squirt or two of whipped cream and grated nutmeg.

NOTE:

To ring the changes you can add 1 shot of hot espresso and reduce the milk by 30 ml/1 oz. or add 30 ml/1 oz. cold brew coffee to the saucepan and reduce the milk by 30 ml/1 oz.

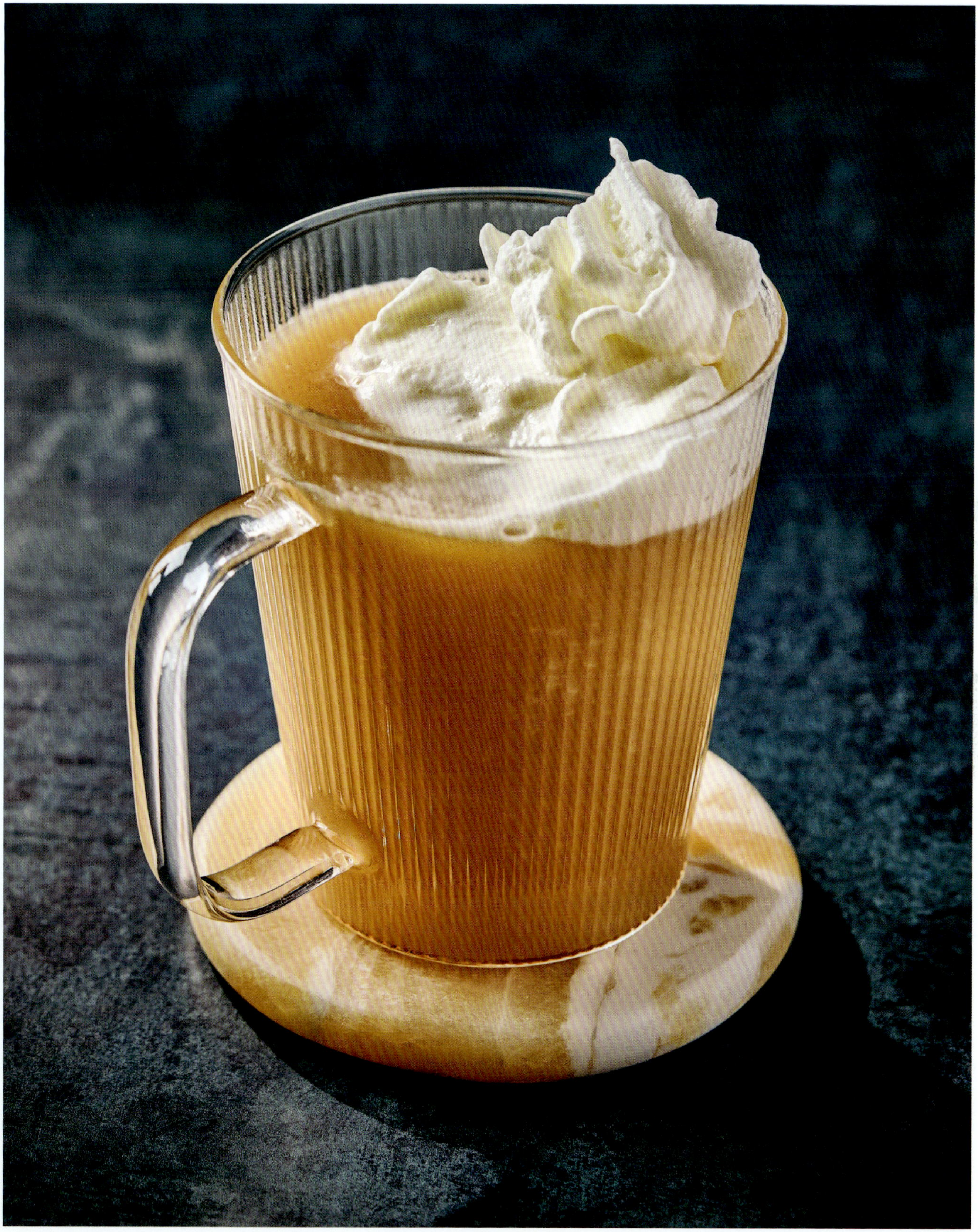

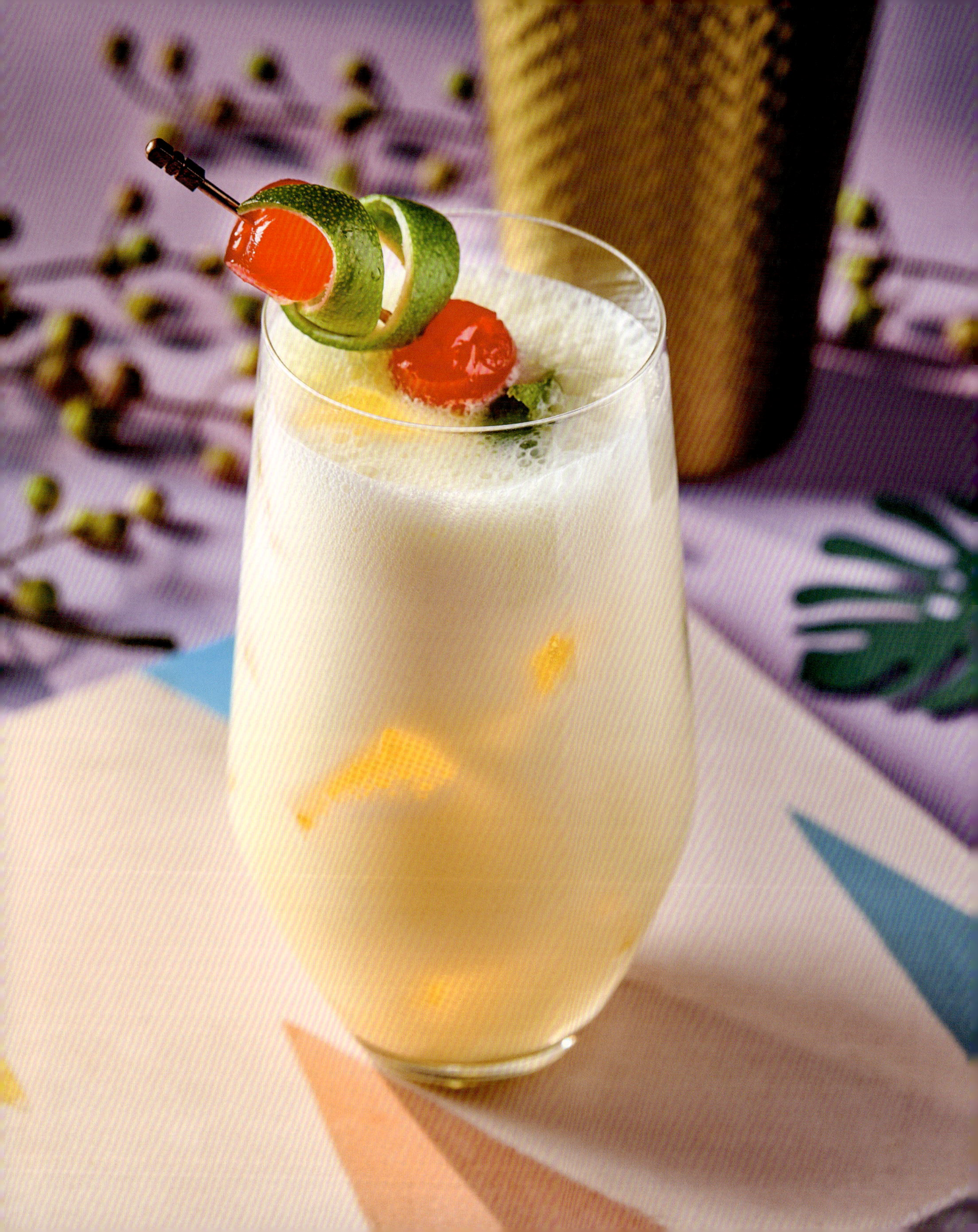

SNOWBELL

Why not swap your seasonal retro Snowball cocktail for this Snowbell? The boozy Advocaat is replaced with a pre-made custard for a similarly satisfying concoction.

30 ml/1 oz. cold pre-made custard
1 teaspoon rum cake flavouring
squeeze of lime juice
100 ml/3½ oz. clear sparkling lemonade
cocktail cherry and lime zest, to garnish

SERVES 1

Shake the custard and rum flavouring with ice, strain into a tall ice-filled glass, add a squeeze of lime juice and top up with sparkling lemonade. Garnish with a cocktail cherry and a wedge of lime.

BASIC RECIPES

Many of these syrups are now available to buy off-the-shelf, but if they are not available, or if you prefer a more home-made feel, here are some reliable basic recipes.

SIMPLE SUGAR SYRUP

200 g/1 cup white granulated sugar
250 ml/1 cup water

Combine the sugar and water in a clean bottle with a tight-fitting lid and shake well. Occasionally shake until the sugar has dissolved. Store the syrup in an airtight container in the refrigerator for up to 2 weeks. As long as the ratio is the same, you can increase or decrease the quantities.

RICH SIMPLE SUGAR SYRUP

200 g/1 cup Demerara or Turbinado sugar
250 ml/1 cup water

In a small pan heat the sugar and water over medium heat, stirring until the sugar dissolves. Remove from the heat and cool to room temperature. Store the syrup in an airtight container in the refrigerator for up to 2 weeks.

COLD BREW COFFEE SYRUP

250 ml/1 cup cold brew coffee
200 g/1 cup Demerara or Turbinado sugar

In a medium saucepan bring the ingredients to the boil, stirring to dissolve. Lower the heat to a simmer, stirring often. Let cool to room temperature. Store in an airtight container in the refrigerator for up to 1 month.

COFFEE SYRUP

180 ml/¾ cup water
1 cinnamon stick
200 g/1 cup Demerara or Turbinado sugar
4 tablespoons medium-coarse ground coffee, preferably a fruity Ethiopian or Kenyan blend
¼ teaspoon pure vanilla extract
1 star anise

In a small saucepan, combine the water with the cinnamon over medium heat, and bring to the boil. Whisk in the sugar, coffee and vanilla, then turn the heat down to low and simmer gently for 5 minutes. Add the star anise, stir the mixture once, and remove from the heat. Let cool to room temperature; about 45 minutes.

Fine-strain the mixture, pressing on the solids to extract as much liquid as possible (discard the solids). Store the syrup in an airtight container in the refrigerator for up to 2 weeks.

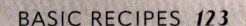

BASIC RECIPES

CHOCOLATE SYRUP

30 g/1 oz. unsweetened cocoa powder
600 g/3 cups granulated white sugar
500 ml/2 cups water
¾ teaspoon vanilla extract
60 ml/2 oz. cinnamon syrup (optional)

In a saucepan heat the cocoa powder, sugar and water over medium–high heat, bring to the boil and stir gently for 3 minutes. Cool to room temperature, then add the vanilla and cinnamon syrup, if needed. Store the syrup in an airtight container in the refrigerator for up to 1 month.

VANILLA SYRUP

200 g/1 cup granulated white sugar
250 ml/1 cup water
1 vanilla pod/bean, split lengthways

In a small saucepan, add the sugar and water and combine over a medium heat, stirring until the sugar dissolves. Remove from heat, add the vanilla bean, and let cool to room temperature.

Strain, cover, and keep refrigerated for up to 2 weeks.

HONEY SYRUP

250 ml/1 cup runny honey
250 ml/1 cup water

In a small saucepan, add the honey and water and mix over a medium heat, stirring until the honey has dissolved. Remove from heat and allow to cool to room temperature. Store the syrup in an airtight container in the refrigerator for up to 2 weeks

GINGER SYRUP

170 g/1 cup unpeeled, washed, fresh ginger root, roughly chopped
200 g/1 cup granulated white sugar
750 ml/3 cups water

Process the ginger chunks in a food processor or blender until finely chopped. Place in a large saucepan, add the sugar and water, and stir. Bring to the boil then reduce the heat, allowing the mixture to simmer over medium-low heat. Cook for 1 hour until a rich syrup is created. Strain the syrup twice through cheesecloth or a fine sieve/strainer. Keep refrigerated for up to 2 weeks.

CINNAMON SYRUP

200 g/1 cup granulated white sugar
250 ml/1 cup water
4 'true' cinnamon sticks (rather than cassia), broken into large chunks

Bring all ingredients to a boil in a small pan set over over medium heat. Reduce and let simmer for 8–10 minutes, stirring frequently. Remove from the heat and let cool. Strain, discard the cinnamon sticks, and cover. Keep refrigerated for up to 2 weeks.

CITRIC ACID SOLUTION

10 g/⅓ oz. citric acid powder
100 ml/3¾ oz. water

For a 10% solution, mix the citric acid powder with the water. Whisk until the citric acid is dissolved. Bottle the solution and keep refrigerated for up to 3 months.

SALINE SOLUTION

80 ml/2¾ oz. filtered water
20 g/⅔ oz. sea salt (such as Maldon)

For a 20% solution, mix the water and salt well, then pass through a coffee filter to remove any insoluble bits. Fill a small glass dropper bottle with a pipette, for use in small quantities.

HOMEMADE VANILLA COFFEE CREAMER

25 g/¾ oz. coffee creamer or single/light cream
1 teaspoon vanilla syrup (see page 124)

Combine the ingredients in a small cup or jug/pitcher and stir. Use as needed. This will keep for up to 48 hours when covered and refrigerated.

INDEX

agave syrup: Daisy, Daisy 30
Agua de Sandía 54
Agua Fresca 54
Almave Blanco: Daisy, Daisy 30
   The Dove 29
   Tropical Sunrise 29
Amaretto Sour, Pineapple 21
America-No 25
Angostura Bitters & Tonic 66
apple juice: Fruit Punch 39
   Hot Buttered Apple 112
   Mulled Cider 111
Arnold Palmer 69

B
Banana Batida 43
   Peanut Butter Banana Batida 43
Big T Time 65
Black Satin 96
blue fruit juice: Something Blue 40
Boston Cooler 82
Bucks Fizz 22
Butterscotch, Hot 116
   Sweater Weather Hot Butterscotch 116

C
Cafe de Shannon 91
Chai Tea Latte 115
   Coconut Chai Tea 115
   Vanilla Chai Latte 115
Chamomile Collins 61
Cherry Cola 78
   Chocolate-Covered Cherry Cola 100
cherry juice: Fruit Punch 39
Cherry Pie 86
cherry syrup 78
   Cherryade 58
Chocolate Bitters & Lemon-Lime Soda 66
chocolate milk: Espresso Love 95
   Frozen Hot Chocolate 120
chocolate syrup 124
   Chocolate-Covered Cherry Cola 100
   Chocolate Egg Cream 77
   Egg Custard Tart 86
   Phosphate Soda 81
cinnamon syrup 124

citric acid solution 125
coconut cream: Coconut Chai Tea 115
   The Virgin Colada 40
coconut milk: Banana Batida 43
coconut water: Something Blue 40
coffee: Cafe de Shannon 91
   Coffee and Cereal 103
   Coffee & Soda 85
   coffee syrup 123
   cold brew coffee syrup 123
   Dirty Horchata 99
   Espresso Love 95
   Kaffe & Tonic 92
   Shakerato 103
coffee creamer, vanilla 125
coffee ice cream: Coffee Cabinet 85
cola: Cherry Cola 78
   Chocolate-Covered Cherry Cola 100
   Coke & Rum 34
   Dirty Cola 100
   Orange Bitters & Cola 66
   Red-Eye Special 100
   Roy Rogers 13
   Spezi 62
   Trigger 13
condensed milk: Banana Batida 43
   Iced Hong Kong Milk Tea 104
   Red-Eye Special 100
Cool Mint Frappé 61
cornflake-infused milk: Coffee and Cereal 103
Cottage Garden Cup 53
cranberry juice: Cranberry Fizz 48
   Tea by the Sea 47
cream: Cafe de Shannon 91
   Chai Tea Latte 115
   Dirty Cola 100
   Vanilla Chai Latte 115
cream soda: Popstar Pop 26
cucumber: Agua Fresca de Pepino 54
   Cottage Garden Cup 53
   Double Mint Lime Soda 70
   Salty Cucumber Lime Soda 70
custard: Cherry Pie 86
   Egg Custard Tart 86
   Snowbell 119

D
Daiquiri, The Driver's 17
Daisy, Daisy 30

Dirty Cola 100
Dirty Horchata 99
Dirty Martini 21
Double Mint Lime Soda 70
The Dove 29
The Driver's Daiquiri 17
Duke of Earl 33

E F
Earl Grey tea: Duke of Earl 33
Easy Being Green 65
Egg Creams 77
Egg Custard Tart 86
Espresso Love 95
Fanta, Spezi 62
Frappe, Cool Mint 61
French 7.5 33
Frozen Hot Chocolate 120
fruit: Fruit Egg Cream 77
   Fruit Punch 39
fruit syrups: Phosphate Soda 81

G
gin substitute: Dirty Martini 21
   French 7.5 33
   Martini 21
   No-Groni 25
   Popstar Martini 26
   Tonic & Gin 34
ginger: Chai Tea Latte 115
   ginger syrup 124
   Gingered Limonana 73
   Mulled Wine 111
   Vanilla Chai Latte 115
ginger ale: Boston Cooler 82
   Presbyterian 57
ginger beer: Cottage Garden Cup 53
   Grey 'n' Windy 18
gingerbread syrup: Sweater Weather Hot Butterscotch 116
grape juice: Supersonic 48
grapefruit juice: The Dove 29
   Grapefruit Radler 62
green tea: Easy Being Green 65
   see also matcha
grenadine: Roy Rogers 13
   Shirley Temple 13
   Trigger 13
Grey 'n' Windy 18
Guinness (Irish dark stout): Black Satin 96

H
Hibiscus Lemonade 59
   Patti Borg 69
High Tide Daiquiri 17

honey syrup 124
   Hot Toddy 112
   Matcha Latte 107
Hong Kong Milk Tea 104
Horchata 99
   Dirty Horchata 99
   Pink Horchata 99
Hot Buttered Apple 112
Hot Butterscotch 116
   Sweater Weather Hot Butterscotch 116
Hot Chocolate, Frozen 120
Hot Toddy 112

I
ice cream: Boston Cooler 82
   Coffee Cabinet 85
Iced Strawberry Matcha Latte 107
iced tea: Iced Hong Kong Milk Tea 104
   Island-style iced teas 44
   Tea by the Sea 47
   Tea Tonic 48
Island-style iced teas 44

J K
Just the Tonic 48
Kaffe & Tonic 92

L
lager, non-alcoholic: Big T Time 65
   Grapefruit Radler 62
Lattes: Chai Tea Latte 115
   Vanilla Chai Latte 115
lemon juice: Chamomile Collins 61
   Cherryade 58
   Chocolate-Covered Cherry Cola 100
   Easy Being Green 65
   French 7.5 33
   Gingered Limonana 73
   Grapefruit Radler 62
   Hot Toddy 112
   Lemonade 58
   Mint Limonana 73
   Orangeade 59
   Pineapple Amaretto Sour 21
   Popstar Martini 26
   Watermelon Limonana 73
lemon-lime soda, Chocolate Bitters & 66
lemon soda: Sgroppino 22
Lemonade 58–9
   Arnold Palmer 69

Hibiscus Lemonade 59
Matcha Palmer 69
Pineapple Amaretto Sour 21
Snowbell 119
Stop the Presses 57
lime juice: Agua de Sandía 54
   Agua Fresca de Pepino 54
   Banana Batida 43
   Cranberry Fizz 48
   Daisy, Daisy 30
   Dirty Cola 100
   Double Mint Lime Soda 70
   The Driver's Daiquiri 17
   Fruit Punch 39
   Grey 'n' Windy 18
   Limeade 58
   Mango Tango 47
   Nimbu Sour 70
   Salty Cucumber Lime Soda 70
   Trigger 13
   Virgin Mary 14
Limeade 58
limes: Mocktail Mojito 17
Limonana 73
Lyre's Aperitivo: America-No 25
Lyre's Italian Orange: No-Groni 25
   Sbagliato 25
Lyre's non-alcoholic American Malt: Cafe de Shannon 91
Lyre's White Cane Spirit: The Driver's Daiquiri 17

M N

Mango Tango 47
Martini 21
   Dirty Martini 21
   Popstar Martini 26
Martini Vibrante: America-No 25
matcha: Iced Strawberry Matcha Latte 107
   Matcha Latte 107
   Matcha Palmer 69
milk: Chocolate Egg Cream 77
   Coffee Egg Cream 77
   Coffee Milk 85
   Dirty Horchata 99
   Fruit Egg Cream 77
   Horchata 99
   Iced Strawberry Matcha Latte 107
   Matcha Latte 107
   Pink Horchata 99
   Sweater Weather Hot Butterscotch 116
   Vanilla Egg Cream 77

milk, cornflake-infused: Coffee and Cereal 103
mint: Cottage Garden Cup 53
   Gingered Limonana 73
   Mint Limonana 73
   Mocktail Mojito 17
   Watermelon Limonana 73
mint syrup: Double Mint Lime Soda 70
mint tea: Cool Mint Frappé 61
Mocktail Mojito 17
Mulled Cider 111
Mulled Wine 111
Nimbu Sour 70
No-Groni 25

O

olive juice/brine: Dirty Martini 21
Orange Bitters & Cola 66
Orange Fanta: Spezi 62
orange juice: Big T Time 65
   Bucks Fizz 22
   Fruit Punch 39
   Orangeade 59
   Sunshine Tonic 48
   Tea by the Sea 47
   Tropical Iced Tea 44
   Tropical Sunrise 29
Orangeade 59

P

passion fruit juice: Popstar Martini 26
passion fruit juice drink: Fruit Punch 39
Patti Borg 69
peach iced tea: Tea by the Sea 47
Peanut Butter Banana Batida 43
Phosphate Sodas 81
pineapple juice: Fruit Punch 39
   Pineapple Amaretto Sour 21
   Popstar Martini 26
   Tropical Sunrise 29
   The Virgin Colada 40
pineapple syrup: Tropical Iced Tea 44
Pink Horchata 99
Popstar Martini 26
Popstar Pop 26
Presbyterian 57

R

Red-Eye Special 100
red wine, non-alcoholic: Mulled Wine 111

rice milk, unsweetened 99
   Dirty Horchata 99
   Horchata 99
   Pink Horchata 99
rich simple sugar syrup 123
Roy Rogers 13
Ruby Rush 17
rum: Coke & Rum 34

S

salt: saline solution 125
   salty cucumber lime soda 70
Sbagliato 25
Sgroppino 22
Shakerato 103
Shirley Temple 13
simple sugar syrup 123
Snowbell 119
soda: Shirley Temple 13
soda water: Coffee & Soda 85
   Double Mint Lime Soda 70
   Egg Custard Tart 86
   Mocktail Mojito 17
   Nimbu Sour 70
   Phosphate Sodas 81
   Presbyterian 57
   Salty Cucumber Lime Soda 70
Something Blue 40
Spezi 62
Stop the Presses 57
strawberries: Cottage Garden Cup 53
   Iced Strawberry Matcha Latte 107
strawberry syrup: Iced Strawberry Matcha Latte 107
   Pink Horchata 99
sugar syrups: rich simple sugar syrup 123
   simple sugar syrup 123
Sunshine Tonic 48
Supersonic 48
Sweater Weather Hot Butterscotch 116
syrups: cherry syrup 78
   chocolate syrup 124
   cinnamon syrup 124
   coffee syrup 123
   cold brew coffee syrup 123
   ginger syrup 124
   honey syrup 124
   rich simple sugar syrup 123
   simple sugar syrup 123
   vanilla syrup 124

T

tea: Arnold Palmer 69

Big T Time 65
Cold Brew Black Tea 104
Cottage Garden Cup 53
Duke of Earl 33
Grey 'n' Windy 18
Iced Hong Kong Milk Tea 104
Island-style iced teas 44
Patti Borg 69
Tea by the Sea 47
Tea Tonic 48
see also green tea; matcha
Toddy, Hot 112
tomato juice: Virgin Mary 14
tonic water: Angostura Bitters & Tonic 66
   Just the Tonic 48
   Kaffe & Tonic 92
   Tonic & Gin 34
Trigger 13
Tropical Iced Tea 44
Tropical Sunrise 29

V

vanilla: Vanilla Chai Latte 115
   vanilla syrup 124
vanilla coffee creamer: Chocolate-Covered Cherry Cola 100
vanilla ice cream: Boston Cooler 82
vanilla powder: Dirty Horchata 99
   Horchata 99
   Pink Horchata 99
Velvet Daiquiri 17
vermouth, non-alcoholic: Dirty Martini 21
   Martini 21
vermouth substitute: No-Groni 25
Versin Aperitivo: Sbagliato 25
The Virgin Colada 40
Virgin Mary 14

W

water, sparkling: America-No 25
watermelon: Agua de Sandía 54
   Watermelon Iced Tea 44
   Watermelon Limonana 73
wine, non-alcoholic: Black Satin 96
   Bucks Fizz 22
   Duke of Earl 33
   French 7.5 33
   Mulled Wine 111
   Sbagliato 25
   Sgroppino 22

ACKNOWLEDGEMENTS

The authors would like to acknowledge Sara L. Smith, without whom the book would not be possible, as well as: all the (soda) jerks past and present, Queenie, Big T, DWS & JPS, Dot & Pete, Michelle & Jim Rivers, Sally & Andrew, Josh 'Muddy' Rivers, Diamond Ken & Bruce, Jellybean, Lara, Jara & Jamjar, Bobby C, Rosie the Bear, Harry 'Skylink' Waterman, Mavis, The Bear & The Cubs, Laura Willoughby and the team at Club Soda, Gin Miller, Josh Kelly, Jeff Bear & Louise, Julesy, Mr & Mrs Jeffers, Rosie Lees, The Hayman Family, Tom & Tina of Warner's, Rachel Sutherland, Dickie, Claire Warner, EZ & The Zandonas, AK, Stupot, Gambler, BP, Dr. Damo & Lil' Ru, Scottish Jamie, Compo & Jersey Rich, VP, VK, Za, D.A.B., SG1, C-Dog, Lorro, Lol Patzy, Toby, The Ausloos', Dave Smith (the other one), Adam Smithson, Sarah Mitchell, Clayton & Ali Hartley, Bill & Erik Owens, Anita & Paragraph, The Spirits Business, IWSC, Foxzilla, Zahra, Chanta, Flashdance Nance & Jason, Lauren Van Cleave, Allie 'The Big Cheese' Klug, Kellie & Finn, Sassy Chasse, Simon Brooking, Steph's Fur Coats, Gardner, Daydream Jones, Jonathan Armstrong, Kay Quigley, Ugo, The Donkeys, Janice Snowden, my disco dancing partners Janice Bailon and Suzu, The Gin Girl, Josh & Joey, The Hotsy Totsy, Wine Shop, Happy Accidents, Best Intentions, Tin Widow, UnderCotê, and every excellent no and low cocktail out there – my kidneys and liver thank you!

We would both also like to thank the shoot team for the beautiful images, photographer Tim Atkins, drinks stylist Katherine Lunt and prop stylist Luis Peral.

And last, but by no means least, our publisher, Julia Charles and the rest of the team at Ryland, Peters & Small; creative director Leslie Harrington, senior designer Toni Kay, copy editor Kate Reeves-Brown and production manager Gordana Simakovic.

PHOTOGRAPHY CREDITS

All photography by Tim Atkins with the following exceptions.

Alex Luck *Pages 17, 21, 26, 33, 34, 43, 47, 50, 57, 65, 69, 70, 82, 86, 91, 92, 95, 96, 99, 104, 112, 115, 120.*

Kate Whitaker *Page 111.*

Clare Winfield *Pages 14, 116.*

ADOBE ILLUSTRATION CREDITS

abbydesign *Page 40.*

Brillianata *Page 53, 78.*

Chakraborty *Pages 13, 17, 22, 30, 53, 61, 70, 81, 86, 95, 119.*

MegaShabanov *Page 43.*

Onetime *Page 115*

Simple Line *Page 92.*

Svetlana *Pages 17, 30, 33, 40, 57, 61, 65, 69.*

WinWin *Page 21.*